Tourism in the Third World

Tourism in the Third World

Christian Reflections by
Ron O'Grady

ORBIS BOOKS
Maryknoll, New York 10545

Acknowledgment is gratefully given for permission to reproduce the following photographs:

Page 2 to John Padula
Pages 28 and 40 to Keystone Press
Page 51 to United Fruit Company
Page 58 to WCC

The cartoons on pp. 19, 31, and 45 are the work of the author.

The Catholic Foreign Mission Society of America (Maryknoll) recruits and trains people for overseas missionary service. Through Orbis Books Maryknoll aims to foster the international dialogue that is essential to mission. The books published, however, reflect the opinions of their authors and are not meant to represent the official position of the society.

First published as *Third World Stopover: The Tourism Debate,* No. 12 in the World Council of Churches Risk book series, copyright © 1981 by World Council of Churches, 150, route de Ferney, 1211 Geneva 20, Switzerland

U.S. edition 1982 by Orbis Books, Maryknoll, NY 10545

Typeset in Switzerland and printed and bound in the United States of America.

Library of Congress Cataloging in Publication Data

O'Grady, Ron.
  Tourism in the Third World

  Reprint. Originally published: Third world stopover. Geneva: World Council of Churches, 1981? (The Risk book series; no. 12)
  Bibliography: p.
  1. Tourist trade—Religious aspects—Christianity.
I. Title. II. Series: Risk book series; no. 12.
G155.A10435   1982   261.8'5   82-8227
ISBN 0-88344-507-7 (pbk.)

Table of contents

Introduction

The stunning growth of international tourism in recent years has made it the largest single item of world trade, with budgets running into billions of dollars. Each year new records are broken. In the year 1979, for which we have accurate figures, there were no fewer than 30,778 people who set out every hour of every day to go overseas as tourists. The number of internal tourists would be at least four times that figure.

This huge flow of people is becoming one of the most significant human experiences of our time. The World Tourism Organisation, a group not given to making extravagant statements, claims that within a short time tourism will be "a socio-economic phenomenon capable of exercising decisive influence on the world." By 2000 A.D. it may well be the most important economic activity of the world.

Until recently, the churches had shown little real interest in tourism, beyond the marginal concern related to pilgrimages and holy places. That situation is rapidly changing. Over the past few years, several regional church groups have initiated consultations to deal with aspects of tourism and the responsibility of the churches. These culminated in the International Workshop on Tourism* held in Manila, Philippines, September 12-25, 1980.

The participants at this meeting came predominantly from Asia and the Pacific, but representatives were also present from Africa, the Caribbean, Europe and the United States. It was a fully ecumenical gathering, with a number of Roman Catholic and Protestant action groups from the Philippines also involved in the programme.

The participants had the unique opportunity of meeting with people from across the whole spectrum of the tourist industry. Not only did they have sessions with representatives of government, hotel, airline, and other official tourist agencies; they also went into the provinces and spoke with a widely representative group of ordinary people who have been affected by tourism. They met people who had

---

*See **Third World Tourism**, published by the Christian Conference of Asia, 1980, for the official report of the consultation, and Appendix 1 for the statement.

lost their land, hotel workers and union secretaries, prostitutes and bar girls, boatmen and waiters. In two weeks they became involved with the lives of hundreds of people, and they prepared many documents and statements.

From the Manila meeting has emerged the Ecumenical Coalition for Third World Tourism which seeks to provide a new framework for united action. This group has the official approval of ecumenical regional bodies in Asia, the Pacific and the Caribbean, and it holds great promise for future Christian involvement in tourism.

But why should the church become involved in tourism? That question is often asked, especially in Western countries. In this book I shall try to answer it from a third world perspective. It is important to remember that the concern for tourism has come from churches in Asia, the Pacific and the Caribbean. It is a direct grass-roots challenge. In the affluent West one can accept tourism without too many qualms. But from the slums, villages and settlements of the third world the view is different. This book is written to interpret some of the third world anxieties about tourism, so that a wider audience will begin to understand the issues. It is written for readers with a Christian background, and it tries to deal with specific concerns which would be readily understood by such readers. I hope however that the issues dealt with will be of interest to all people of good will.

The first section of the book deals with the negative effects of rich tourism in poor countries. These are not exaggerated. Many third world people would speak more strongly on the subject than I have spoken here. The second part of the book addresses itself to the basic question of how to make tourism a more positive force for development in poor countries — how to give tourism a 'human face' as Pope Paul once put it.

There is a growing library of books, articles, research monographs and statistical surveys which will support most of the central contentions of this book. We include some of these in Appendix 3.

It should perhaps be made clear that this is not a book about tourism in general. We cannot automatically transpose the stories recounted here to an affluent society.

Here our concern is with the effect of rich tourists entering poor countries. The book does not presume to pass judgements on the ethics of rich tourists travelling in other rich countries or within their own. Such tourism has many positive benefits. But when these same wealthy people visit poor countries a new dynamic enters, and there is a major qualitative difference in the tourism.

Let me add a brief word of explanation. Most of my personal experience has been in Asia, so I have tended to use illustrations from this background. Similar stories are available from third world resort centres in other regions. (Expressions like 'third world' or 'poor' world, however unsatisfactory, form a convenient short-hand.)

Finally, my thanks are due to those who have enabled me to write this book: to the Christian Church (Disciples) who gave me time to complete it; to my friends in the Department of Communication of the World Council of Churches for agreeing to publish it. I must also thank that large community of individuals from third world church agencies who are bound together by their common anxiety about the effects of tourism on their own cultures. They are not responsible for all the ideas in this book, but if tourism ever becomes more humanized, it will be largely due to their pioneering work.

RON O'GRADY

I. Here come the tourists

The tourism industry has been growing at a rate which confounds all predictions. Today it is number one, and still growing. It outstrips oil as the major industry of the world; it employs more people than any other industry. Americans spend more on their leisure than they do on defence. The list of such economic and social indicators is endless. Despite recession, unemployment, oil crises, inflation and political upheavals, tourism continues its upward march undaunted.

Until recently, this growth had gone unchallenged. A few isolated voices were raised about some of the social consequences of unchecked tourism, but these had little significant impact. The industry continued to generate such enormous wealth and engage in such profligate spending that countries in search of economic independence and development had accepted tourism with undisguised enthusiasm.

But not any longer. Now questions are being raised. Countries which had fallen over themselves to get a new "Hilton-American Express-Pan Am-Service" are beginning to wonder whether the benefits are as large as were expected. This is particularly true of those poor countries which are the focus of this book. Many are now expressing reservations about certain aspects of tourism.

To understand why, we must begin with the interaction between people who are poor and their affluent guests.

Consider the poor. They are people who will never be tourists. When they speak of travel they mean going on foot, or in a crowded bus, to the next village or town. Possibly they will travel for a wedding, a funeral, or some religious festival, but their travel will not be for pleasure. Family incomes are barely sufficient for survival and there is no extra money available for luxury travel. Indeed, when they think of luxury, their minds cannot stretch far beyond a bottle of soft drink or a better meal. The concept of a paid holiday or expenditure on leisure travel or visiting a foreign culture is totally outside their conceptual framework.

Into the land of the poor come the tourists. At first came only a few courageous people, usually sensitive in their attitude to other peoples and other cultures. They were rewarded with all the courtesy and hospitality of traditional societies. Then the numbers increase and improved facilities for travel are required. Surveys are made of possible tourist resorts and great profits are projected. The host community is persuaded that tourism will bring the blessings of employment and of foreign funds and promote the development of natural resources — all for the good of the whole community. The contracts are signed, the money slips under the counter, the jumbo jets begin to fly in, and there is a major qualitative change in the life of the whole society.

Consider now the new arrivals. They represent a growing international community, with more money than they can spend on their daily needs, and they are thus able to spend on international travel. Ninety per cent of these travellers still go to other developed nations. Western and Southern Europe and America remain the favourite destinations. But the ten per cent who travel each year to third world countries represent about 30 million people, and the number increases every year.

Not all the tourists are rich people in their own country. An increasing number come from lower middle-class communities and often are those who perform quite menial tasks in their home-land. Workers in the industrialized na-

Keystone-Press

tions increasingly demand the right to have paid holidays every year. It is estimated that about 500 million working people now receive an annual paid holiday. This means that the modern tourist class is made up of farmers and factory workers, secretaries and plumbers. Given the generous unemployment benefits in some welfare states, even the unemployed can become tourists today.

While many tourists are thus simple working-class people in their home country, when they travel overseas, they suddenly become rich. For the first time in their life, they have others to serve them, make their beds, drive them in private cars, massage their back and serve their every whim. The new extravagant lifestyle becomes possible only because of the economic disparity between the two countries. So while the tourists often live very humbly in their home environment, they become the new rich in the host country. For many it is a heady experience which can quickly become addictive.

When such a tourist group visits an affluent country, the possibility of friction is much less. A common cultural history, similar social values and shared languages facilitate communication. Equally important is the fact that the host country has all the facilities normally demanded by tourists. An adequate infrastructure of communication, travel, hygiene and food distribution means that the coming of the tourist does not disturb local conditions. Tourism in these countries began as internal tourism and only slowly evolved into an international exchange. The rough edges were smoothed on the way.

Poorer nations lack this infrastructure. They are asked to make the leap from a predominantly rural-based economy into a service-oriented tourist nation without passing through an intermediate stage of industrialization. Money is diverted from social projects to build roads and bridges to serve the tourist; drainage facilities are inadequate, and so raw sewerage is pumped into the sea; the electrification of villages is postponed because of the need to have air-conditioning, elevators and similar amenities in hotels; increased demand for certain types of food and consumer goods by tourists raises the price of these goods in the local market; money which is needed for housing, health care, schools and agricultural development is diverted to meet the ever-increasing needs of a foreign elite.

Although we are focusing on tourism in this discussion, it should not be inferred that tourism is the central or only problem. Every poor nation struggles to improve the living conditions of its people. With or without tourism, this is the central issue for human development. What tourism does is to inject a false hope into such struggling communities. The assumption that this new industry will automatically improve the situation of the poor is a false one. Although there is certainly economic benefit to sections of the host community and many new jobs are generated, the overall improvement in the living standard of the people is much less than is claimed. Indeed, in some areas of social life, the developing nation may lose more than it gains. Tourism is not a magic wand which will solve a nation's ills and there are situations in which these ills will even be compounded.

II. The mobile ghetto

The tourist group

To leave the relative comfort of an affluent society for the first time and to travel alone to a poor country requires considerable courage. The fear of the unknown is very strong. Without local contacts and a knowledge of local language or customs, the traveller will feel helpless. It is understandable, then, that the largest single part of tourism to underdeveloped nations is the mass tour. Whether we call it group tour, package tour or charter tour, the effect is the same: large numbers of people programmed to move simultaneously across the landscape at a given time.

To the tourist, this kind of travel has the attraction of safety. It is also cheaper than travelling on one's own. The tourism industry has compelling reasons to encourage such tourism because it is easier to organize thirty people travelling together than to try and handle thirty individuals. The competition for this type of tourist has become greatly intensified and, since it further reduces prices, we can look forward to increasing numbers of mass tours criss-crossing the skies in jumbo jets.

In many quarters the group tour has been a source of amusement and the theme of films and novels. The actual nature of the group tour experience has, however, received little attention. There are five aspects of such tourism which have particular relevance to our theme.

1. The dynamics of a group tour are such that the prime relationships are always those that occur within the group itself. The group normally numbers at least 15 people and can often be very much larger. These diverse individuals, thrown together for the first time, must determine their place within the group and create their own sub-groups of interest. The fact that they go through certain shared experiences gives a sense of group solidarity, but there are also times when the strain of working out inter-group tensions and differences is considerable.

The result of this inter-action will be to insulate the group from either the need or the desire to establish significant relations with the host community. There is enough emotional heat within the group itself and this means that encounters beyond its confines will be brief and impersonal.

2. The orientation of group tourism is so much towards enjoyment or hedonism that members will avoid the possibility of having a real relationship with the host community. They willingly accept the spectator role. They are voyeurs of the society they pass through.

When the host country is poor, a group tour gives little chance for its members to understand the factors which underlie this poverty. Insulated in air-conditioned coaches, they can photograph poverty from afar. They may get upset by the persistence of the beggars, but they will be unable to explore the way in which this particular society has created so many victims.

Forced into the role of spectators, they must fall back on uninformed and conventional wisdom to explain it away. They will give the beggar a few coins, one way of avoiding the issue. They will assume that there are easy solutions to the problem which their own country's know-how would have found. Their discussion of poverty is as a rule full of patronizing and racist cliches.

3. It follows that the group tour reinforces prejudice rather than changes it. A white tourist who leaves home with the assumption that certain coloured races are inferior will in all probability return unchallenged and unchanged. The contact with the host community will usually be confined to shopkeepers, service personnel and beggars. The aim of the shopkeeper and the beggar is to make as much money as possible at the expense of the tourist, and the relationship is like a chess match with each trying to outdo the other. In the case of the service industries the tourist has the advantage of being able to tip or to withhold a tip. It is the hope of a generous tip, together with the fear of losing their job, which makes the service staff obliging, servile, polite and pleasant.

Such relationships will not challenge the prejudices or assumptions of the tourists. If the tour gives them the opportunity to confront intellectuals, labour leaders, religious, community workers, radicalized students or peasant groups, it is possible that they would be forced to revise their opinions, but such contacts are not part of the itinerary of the usual group tour. It is largely true that the group tour passes through a poor country without encountering the realities of that country.

4. The more they are threatened by the local culture, the more the members of the group will retreat into their own provincialisms. In most travel there are forms of culture shock. The group tour does its best to insulate its members from such disturbances but, even so, the external world keeps intruding in a manner which upsets the tour group. Except in rare instances, the group will not be able to work through the issues in a creative way; it will only have recourse to recognized patterns of behaviour. In the hotel bars of India we find Australian men acting as if they were in a macho pub in Australia; in the lounge bars of Hong Kong the Americans speak of the baseball season in Chicago. Retreat to an excessive nationalism is a mechanism by which the group avoids the awkward questions which a poor society keeps throwing up.

5. The style of operation of the group domesticates the participants and prevents them from exploring an alien culture in a meaningful way. When Japanese tourists go abroad they follow the tour leader's flag in disciplined and obedient rows. They understand the rules of the game — which is to see as many well-known 'tourist' sights as possible and to have their photo taken in front of each one. While other national groups do not act in such a regimented fashion, they too find themselves being just as much tamed by the group tour. The compulsion to rush into every temple to look at the statue of a well-known Buddha is so strong that the group lets itself be intimidated by the time-table. The critical faculties are suspended and the group allows itself to be driven from place to place, stopping only to eat at designated restaurants and shop at special bargain stores, not knowing that the prices in both places are inflated to cover the kick-backs. The tourist itinerary turns otherwise sensitive and critical people into a flock of sheep.

When all these dynamics are put together, we are led to the conclusion that the group tour exists as a thing apart from the society. The tour is a form of mobile ghetto passing through the poor countries but not in contact with the real essence of the place. Not only are the tourists mobile, they are also rich, and their wealth effectively insulates them from the agony and the anger of the under-privileged and marginalized sections of the society.

The host community

Let us now reverse the lens on our study and try to see the tourist from the perspective of the host community. The reactions of those who directly serve the tourists in hotels and tourist centres are inevitably mixed, with self-interest, envy and frustration playing a part. But what about other people?

At one end, there is the passive but amused tolerance which is summarized by Senator Jose Diokno of the Philippines. He claims that the stereotyped picture which local people have of a tourist

> is that of a good-natured, rather bumbling, foreigner who comes to this country with a camera slung around his neck and who walks along our streets, kind of gawking at what he sees or rides in air-conditioned buses which very, very few of our people can afford to ride in.[1]

The tourist as a figure of fun appears in cartoons and folk drama. Such images are normally unflattering to the countries concerned.

But this is only one reaction. In many of the highly politicized nations of the third world, the tourist is seen as symbolic of a neo-imperialism which, in new and subtle ways, threatens the integrity of the country's independent stand. Often this reaction erupts in anger, and many tourist resorts have had to get police help to put down outbursts against tourists. The protest poet Cecil Rajendra who lives in Malaysia's most popular tourist destination, Penang Island, writes in strong words:

> When the tourists flew in
> our island people
> metamorphosed into
> a grotesque carnival
> — a two-week sideshow

When the tourists flew in
our men put aside
their fishing nets
to become waiters
our women became whores

When the tourists flew in
what culture we had
flew out of the window
we traded our customs
for sunglasses and pop
we turned sacred ceremonies
into ten-cent peep shows

When the tourists flew in
local food became scarce
prices went up
but our wages stayed low

When the tourists flew in
we could no longer
go down to our beaches
the hotel manager said
"Natives defile the sea-shore"

When the tourists flew in
the hunger and the squalour
were preserved
as a passing pageant
for clicking cameras
— a chic eye-sore!

When the tourists flew in
we were asked
to be 'side-walk ambassadors'
to stay smiling and polite
to always guide
the 'lost' visitor...
Hell, if we could only tell them
where we really want them to go![2]

In the pages of newspapers in the developing world we
come across the same kind of response from many sections
of the community. Dr Vinayak Purohit of India writes:

Rich foreign visitors affect our social life adversely. They provide a glaring example of easy and worldly success. Our youth and children are being corrupted by their lifestyle. The State should not pamper these rich. They must not be allowed to import special goods and drink, they should not be allowed to move about in air-conditioned cars, there should not be any first-class in our civil aviation.[3]

The contrast between the rich and the poor is discovered in every kind of tourism on each continent. In Africa where the popular form of tourism is to imprison humans in buses so they can see animals which are free, the game warden at Serengeti Park writes:

The heart of the problem is the poverty of my African brothers and the terrible wealth of the tourists. African drivers are constantly being tipped to break the rules of our Park and chase the animals. What can you do? Our people are poor. It is easy for them to be corrupted.[4]

To young people in simple island societies, the complexity of tourism brings added threat:

No one can see the sky nowdays
when I stay Waikiki
Get buildings every place I look
More taller than one tree
I think so now they got too much
hotels in Waikiki
dat's why I say Ol'Molokai
is just the place for me.[5]

The poorer the host society the stronger are the challenges made to traditional lifestyles by mass tourism. The ethical dilemma is well stated by Bouhdiba:

Tourism injects the behaviour of a wasteful society in the midst of a society of want. What the average tourist consumes in Tunisia in a week, in the way of meat, butter, dairy products, fruit and pastries, is equivalent to what two or three Tunisians eat in a whole year. The rift between rich and poor societies at this point is no longer an academic issue but an everyday reality.[6]

On the streets, tourism has become an everyday and central discussion point in many developing countries. The changes it brings are both subtle and blatant and in the markets and villages alike some of these changes are being noted and give cause for concern.

The tourist offers an immediate and visible target for the general anger of the people. If there is frustration over the lack of economic development and if this is seen to be related to American foreign policy, then American tourists are a convenient group to attack. This warns us against analysing tourism in isolation from the wider economic development.

Yet it is our contention that tourism in many countries is not only the symbol of 'anti-development', it is also a cause. In the following chapters we shall examine some of the evidence which leads to this conclusion.

Alternative tourists

When local people express their anger at tourists, they usually refer to the group tourists. There are, however, many other kinds of tourism. The tourism industry has many lists of classification. There are those who travel in pursuit of hobbies or sports, who follow professional interests, attend conferences or relax between business calls. We shall discuss some of these groups later. Since they do not usually bring out anxiety in the local population we will not introduce them here.

There is however, one significant group of travellers who need special mention. This group of tourists has no special designation. In developing countries they are usually 'hippies'. Writers call them alternative tourists, drifters, or they are known by descriptive names like 'lumpen bohemia.'[7]

They are the large number of (mostly) young people coming from the affluent societies who explore the third world in an unstructured manner, trying to identify with the local stream of life. With no fixed itinerary, they remain in one place until they decide to move on to another place. Because they are not always well-received by the local people they tend to follow fairly well-defined trails. The underground of the movement has its own communication system which enables the group to identify certain hotels and centres which have shown tolerance to the lifestyle of the travellers.

Part of the mythology of the group is that they should travel as cheaply as possible. To this extent they have some possibility of identifying with the poor sections in developing nations. At least they learn more than they would in a five-star hotel. However they are always insulated against the worst effects of poverty by their ability to send a telegram to their family asking for money. They are convinced that their experience in poor countries is 'authentic' and are always anxious to compare this with that of other tourists.

In any analysis of tourism these alternative tourists must be taken seriously. They remain in one place longer than traditional tourists, they establish quite deep relations with some sections of the local community, especially the young, and they develop a distinctive alternative lifestyle. These three factors seem to indicate that the group of alternative travellers in each city or town directly affects the local culture as profoundly as the mass tourists.

Why do young people travel in this way? Much can be traced to the natural yearning for challenge, adventure and the experience of something different. But for many the motivation can be traced to discontent with their own society. In the current mood of disenchantment with Western culture and economic values, young people of the affluent countries are searching for a society which has more integrity than they perceive in their own country. Like the ancient seekers for the fabled Shangri-la, many of today's young travellers have high ideals and motivation in looking for some meaning behind the mystery of life.

In this process of searching and discovery a few find some religious meaning in life and are changed in a permanent and positive direction. Others develop a love and respect for another culture, and some are disillusioned. Drug addiction is common among those who have been on the trail for a long time. And feelings of racial or ethnic superiority are often evident. Many have taken to certain forms of crime like smuggling, confidence tricks and theft. Quite a number suffer from various kinds of disease.

Third world countries are not as a rule enthusiastic about this group of travellers. An increasing number of countries ban their entry altogether. Some Southeast Asian airports now provide scissors for young men to cut their hair if they wish to enter the country, while the tougher immigration authorities will simply put any youth who doesn't look tidy on the next flight out.

The concern is understandable. Although the mores of the young travellers decree that they should enter the local stream of life, in practice they retain many of the more offensive aspects of alien cultures. The young tourist is often as conservative as older tourists though it shows in different areas.

In Asia and the Pacific Islands, the dress of the alternative tourists causes offence. Increasing numbers of tourists from Northern and Western Europe have come to accept nudity. When it is practised on the beaches of India or Sri Lanka, local residents react with anger. At a popular tourist beach in Sri Lanka recently, a naked young man taking a bath at the village water pump was assaulted by an indignant woman.[8]

Conventional wisdom in the receiving countries associates the 'hippies' with drugs, sexual immorality, loose hygienic standards, crime, laziness and exploitation. There is evidence that all of these are true, in varying degrees. The sense of cynicism and purposelessness which characterizes communities of young people in Katmandhu, Calcutta, Kuta, Phuket and other popular stopping places in Asia is extremely depressing. Newspapers carry regular reports on criminal activities among the young communities.

To local residents it is the demonstration effect which is most upsetting. Unlike mass tourists, the young people are anxious to adopt at least some of the local customs. They are selective at this point, but their enthusiasm to adopt local customs is matched only by that of the local young people to adopt the ways of the West. The local young people are equally selective. The Western values they want to adopt often represent the worst aspects of that culture, and those which are most anti-developmental. Poorer societies could not adopt the leisurely lifestyle of hippy tourists without massive social disruption, and it poses a serious threat to the whole community when the young people begin to ape the easy-going young travellers. The drifter tourists create new social tensions which they are powerless to handle and which do not help the local people.

There are instances when the young people who come as guests are sensitive and open, and even become identified with the struggles of the host community in a real and liberating way. But such instances are rare and, no matter how significant their contribution, they can hardly offset the harm which is done to the social fabric of many poor communities by the presence of such a disturbing force in their midst.

III. Profit and loss

The economics of tourism

For third world governments, the struggle for economic growth is the central and dominating issue. To the citizens of these countries economic justice is a necessity for sheer survival. Given such expectations, on the part of both the people and their rulers, it is not surprising that tourism has been embraced with enthusiasm by the poor nations of the world. Ostensibly it offers to governments the irresistible lure of a quick growth in foreign exchange earnings and, to the people, the promise of much new employment.

There is a case for enthusiasm. Countries can improve their earnings through tourism and new jobs are indeed generated, but it will be our contention in this chapter that many of the claims made for real development are exaggerated, and that the economic benefits are not nearly as large as tourism proponents would like us to believe. We also raise the question as to whether the economic benefits that tourism may bring will actually outweigh the loss that will result in other areas.

Tourism planning

How does international tourism begin in a poor country? It is not surprising that the initiative usually comes from outside the country itself, and that it is presented by tourism interests in an attractive package of statistics and projections.

There is, for example, the popular story of the first visit to Nepal by tourism organizers and their international backers who met with the king of Nepal in the early 1950's. The king was reportedly puzzled, and asked: "Why should anyone want to come here? Why don't they go to Calcutta where there is something to do?" The tourists soon found there was plenty to do in Nepal and the freedom with which entrepreneurs have operated drug circles, casinos and trekking tours has created new social conflicts in the country.

Between 1950 and 1970, international cartels of tour operators, bankers, hotel chains, land developers and transport groups kept looking for new places to market as tourist resorts. In this period, most of the accessible nations of the third world were drawn into the tourist circuit, and they eagerly accepted the tourism package on the basis of its economic promise.

An analysis of tourism in Sri Lanka by Derick Mendis[1] details how tourism began in that country only after US AID commissioned a firm of American travel consultants to draw up a ten-year plan of development for the Sri Lankan travel industry. This was completed in 1967, and the following year the government passed the Tourist Development Act. The plan was an impressive document, with photographs, maps, projections, market research, architectural recommendations, community relations programmes and interpretations of Sri Lankan life.

Mendis has analysed the projections for foreign exchange earnings and found that in the first five years the actual receipts were only 25% of the projected minimum earnings, and during the next five years they varied between 30% and 45% of the estimates. The number of visitors also failed to meet the plan's most conservative estimates. The plan claimed that on reasonable data the number of United States visitors would reach 104,000 in 1976, but the actual total was 7,685 or about 7% of the number projected.[2]

Balancing this miscalculation in one direction, there is the Checchi Report commissioned by the US Department of Commerce and the Pacific Area Travel Association, which claimed in 1958 that tourism in the Pacific and Far East region would quadruple in the following ten years. While the specifics were not always fulfilled, the overall growth of tourism in the region was spectacular and outdid the forecasts. In South-East Asia alone, tourist arrivals increased eighteen-fold between 1960 and 1976.[3]

Foreign exchange?

Tourism does generate foreign exchange growth in developing countries. But how much it produces depends on the way we use the available data. Gross tourism receipt is the figure most frequently cited, especially by those who have a vested interest in tourism.

Such a figure has clear limitations. It has to be balanced against gross tourism expenditures. We should also take note of the fact that the interests of a poor country are not well served if the increase in foreign reserves is squandered by the elites of the country on their own overseas travel.

A study by Prof. Wood of Massachusetts University analyses tourism patterns in South-East Asia. He quotes World Tourism Organisation figures to show that 15 out of 33 underdeveloped countries had a negative balance in their tourism account in 1973, and adds that "it is indicative of the extreme social inequality which characterizes most underdeveloped societies, whose ruling elites have become luxury tourists themselves."[4]

Singapore and Hong Kong are the two shopping 'paradises' of Asia. Duty-free goods abound in both cities, and each has over two million tourists per annum — quite a remarkable figure for such a small area. Both centres have noted that the large spenders do not come from Western countries but are the wealthy tourists of neighbouring underdeveloped countries. In Singapore, the largest per capita spenders are not the Japanese or Americans as one would assume, but the Indonesians. When it is remembered that Indonesia has the lowest income figures for all the ASEAN nations (US$337 in 1978), we are struck by the great disparity between the rich and the poor in that land. Indonesia is one of the countries where the gross tourism payments are higher than the tourism receipts, according to Prof. Wood's study.

Even if the gross receipts are higher than the gross payments, this tells only part of the story. What is called for is the net profit to a country after all the invisibles have been deducted. To discover these figures is almost impossible. Not only are there inadequate statistical data, but there are factors like the effects of private agreements, black market transactions, off-setting payments, and the international arrangements for payments — which make the picture so complex that the actual 'leakage' of tourism income cannot be determined with any certainty.

An illustration of the number of groups and interests involved in each tourist operation will show some of the complexities. Take, for example, the simple case of a Japanese tour party in the Philippines. The tourist will normally make arrangments exclusively through a Japanese agency like the Japan Travel Bureau. The group will fly Japan Air Lines or one of its subsidiaries. The members of the group will go in a Japanese automobile to a hotel which is owned exclusively by Japanese interests. Inside the hotel the elevator, electronic equipment and sound system have all been imported from Japan. The 'local' travel agencies, including the guides, are probably all Japanese who will take the tourists in a Japanese bus to nightclubs and massage parlours owned by Japanese. Since the visitors prefer their own food, they will eat at Japanese-owned restaurants which serve only imported items of Japanese food and Japanese drinks.

This of course is an extreme case, but since Japanese tourists account for the major proportion of tourists to the Philippines, it is a significant illustration. In this scenario one can readily see the possibility of a group of tourists making more money for their own country than for the country they visit. Put another way, there are actually some tours in which the imbalance is so great that the Philippines may even be subsidizing Japan to send tourists, however absurd that may sound. Studies in the Caribbean by economists have shown the same kind of outflow in some detail. Louis Perez asserts that "for each dollar spent in the Commonwealth Caribbean, 77 cents returns in some form to the metropole."[5]

The economic reality of international tourism is that it is controlled from the wealthy sending countries and that it is done for the profit of the companies domiciled in the host country. The gains made by the host country are incidental to the wealth which the industry generates in the sending countries. Each major tourist-generating nation has now developed its own network of airlines, hotels, agencies and personnel whose commitment is not to the host country but to the company in their land of origin. Even the illusion of national ownership which is fostered by the local entrepreneurs taking over a franchise for an organization only means more money leaving the country. To use the name 'Holiday Inn' for a hotel, for example, will cost the local person with the franchise 6% of the total turnover.[6] This is a considerable sum and is drawn without risk to the parent company.

The needs and tastes of the tourists are paramount. It is they who determine how the room will be prepared, whether the air-conditioning is switched on and what is found on the menu. All this requires foreign funds. To meet tourist demands for steak, huge quantities of meat must be imported. For bars to stock all the drinks demanded by the tourists, scotch and vodka and gin must come by the crate-load. The loss in foreign exchange caused by such regular luxury imports cannot be exactly determined, but it should be taken into account when countries calculate the profits of tourism.

Shopping presents another contradiction. The amount each tourist spends on shopping is an important factor for local revenue, since it is assumed that this money not only produces foreign exchange but also encourages local small-scale cottage industry. The assumption, however, needs to be challenged. First, because the tourists tend to spend a large proportion of their shopping dollars on duty-free goods at designated shops. Since these goods are all imported and since the margin of profit to the government is negligible, the benefit cannot be considerable. Second, because tourism souvenirs, which show little artistic merit, are increasingly produced in bulk at factories. Such is the international competition for these souvenirs that it is common even in developing countries to find that the trinkets on the shelf have been mass-produced in Hong Kong, Taiwan or Japan.

One of the intangible effects of tourism is seen in the change of local lifestyle and consumer patterns. This is known as the demonstrator effect. The way tourists dress and eat has an impact on the local population. Slowly it acquires a status image. Local teenagers begin to reject the more sensible dress of their ancestors, and take to the jeans, hats and shoes of the visitors. Food habits change, and soon the towns are opening food chains which sell hamburgers, fried chicken and pizza. The universal success of Coca Cola and Pepsi Cola are signs of this image-making. The tourists also bring more expensive images. A foreign watch, radio or camera becomes a valued status symbol and, as the demand grows, the problems of the poor country become aggravated. Foreign funds needed for medicine and agricultural seeds are diverted to meet the new consumer demands.

Once the door is opened to the tourist industry, it has a way of taking over all decisions. Tax holidays are granted, management and franchise fees are negotiated, land is provided at nominal cost, hotels are given special concessions which enable them to import both luxury goods and even overseas personnel to run them. Eventually the host country is at the point of no return. Without such concessions it cannot attract foreign capital, but in making the concessions it progressively limits the actual profit which the country will make.

In addition to all these, there are additional items of expenditure like advertising in foreign countries, granting special privileges to overseas tour operators, making payments to foreign entertainers and subsidies to airlines. In fact, there are so many variables that it is difficult to determine the extent of foreign exchange earnings made through tourism.

But how much does a country lose through foreign exchange leakage? In some areas estimates can be made. The World Tourism Organisation has done some national studies, and they estimate that a minimum of 40% of the gross hotel revenue goes to pay for imports, interest and profit when the hotel is foreign-owned, and that the figure in many cases exceeds 75% of the revenue.[7] This is a very large figure when it is remembered that it is the gross revenue, and that the net revenue will be very much less.

While the need to build up reserves of foreign exchange is not the whole rationale for tourism, it is nevertheless the argument which is most often cited by those who advocate the expansion of tourism to the third world. It is also the one which governments in these poor countries find most persuasive. Yet a study of available data reveals that the expectations which have been built up are inflated and in some cases illusory.

Employment for the people?

Unemployment and underemployment are the major unresolved social problems of most developing countries. Tourism offers the country a new industry which appears relatively labour-intensive. Not only does it directly create a number of new employment prospects, it also increases the number of subsidiary employment prospects.

This is a positive argument which cannot be lightly dismissed. Any activity which offers ordinary people a chance to obtain a living wage, regular employment and dignity as people must be encouraged. But again we should not be taken in by the ebullient oversell of the tourism advocates. There is need to qualify the claims along three lines:

1. The type of work which tourism offers to the local population is unskilled, low-paid and servile. The industry seeks to employ people as labourers, gardeners, room-maids, baggage carriers, drivers, waitresses, and in related occupations. There can be dignity in this work when it is recognized by both management and the community as an important service. But in a third world country the unskilled workers know that there are hundreds who are queuing up for jobs; they are under constant pressure to conform. The management also knows this and in many cases exploits the workers, demanding long hours of work, total dedication, kick-backs and special favours. The worker who shows any sign of in-

dividuality or who raises questions about working conditions will soon be unemployed and without any union support.

The top-paid employment in the industry often goes to expatriates. Professional workers, consultants and managerial staff are usually imported as part of the cost factor in establishing a new hotel. Even at the level of intermediate skilled labour — as in the installation of electric and electronic facilities — labour is sometimes imported.

2. Few countries have a consistent year-round flow of tourists. They are dependent on large numbers of tourists for short periods of time. In Gambia, only 24% of those employed in tourism areas have their jobs for the full year. Others are employed for just a few months. In Sri Lanka, 20% of hotel workers are employed seasonally.

At least part of the employment generated by tourism must be recognized as partial employment or underemployment.

3. The creation of jobs requires investment and must, therefore, be balanced against alternative investments. Tourism is a heavily capital-intensive operation requiring large funding not just for immediate tourist facilities but also for the back-up requirements of airport services, roads and bridges, sewerage and electrical development and many new facilities. A country which has this amount of capital to invest, or which can get foreign loans, must make some difficult decisions about priorities.

In Sri Lanka, the Mendis study showed that the cost of creating a single job in the tourism sector varied a little regionally, but that it averaged US$5,050 overall. In large-scale heavy industry the cost of creating a single job was $3,250, For small-scale cottage industry a job can be created for as little as $16, but averages about $160.[8]

The decision to concentrate the small national resources of a country in the area of tourism diverts them from alternative forms of investment which could produce greater employment possibilities.

Profit or loss?

Any discussion of the economic factors relating to tourism cannot be pursued outside a review of the total development strategy of a nation. In poor countries where huge numbers of peasants and urban poor are barely able to subsist, the concern for a just economic order and the improvement of living conditions should be the first consideration of any good government. One of the illusions of tourism is that it seems to address itself to this problem directly by providing scarce overseas funds for essential imports and by creating more employment and local capital.

We have already suggested that these claims are inflated. But there is yet another area in which the economic effect of tourism will be felt on national development. This is the surrender of self-determination. A country which wishes to pursue seriously international tourism as a national priority cannot do so without signing over some sovereignty in the control of the industry. Because tourism is by nature an international movement and because it has its economic base in the industrialized Western nations, its maintenance and growth depend largely on transnational corporations. We usually judge the TNCs by their glamorous oil, industrial and shipping industries, but the tourism sector is the fastest growing frontier of their operations.

The TNCs own the airlines and the hotels which make the mass movement of people possible. Their aim is to make profit and they often function independently of the interests of any government. A tourist destination will flourish only to the extent the TNCs promote it and make it develop. The TNCs identify and develop tourist resorts. The managing director of Pan Am in Japan stated in 1973:

> In 1967, Pan Am with a history of pioneering in the Pacific decided Guam could be a good destination for the tourist. Starting with a mere two flights weekly Pan Am actively promoted Guam on the Japanese market ...from virtually zero tourist in 1967, Guam will receive in excess of 200,000 tourists in 1973.[9]

But, like the Lord, the TNCs give and the TNCs take away. In 1976 both Qantas and Air France dropped Tahiti from their through routes, and the former symbol of all that was 'exotic' in the South Pacific found its tourism industry plunging down. The fact that there had been a growing disenchantment in the Islands with the effects of tourism may well have contributed to this change. In the Caribbean, airlines and hotel interests pick up and drop some of the smaller island destinations with regularity.

To join the tourism resort centres, a country must be prepared to hand over to foreign interests some of the decisions which affect its citizens. Those interests may prompt the national government to work in ways which are not always in the best interests of the nation's development. Whether the gains are worth the surrender is a question that cannot be evaded.

IV. A bastardized culture

Bali

Bali is a unique island. Alone in all of the vast archipelago of Indonesia it was able to resist the Islamic wave of conquest in the 14th and 15th centuries. Consequently, it retained the primitive Hinduism of earlier years, so that it remains to this day a remarkable repository of the nation's early history.

When foreign visitors began to discover the charm of this island, they were exposed to its distinctive way of life. Anthropologists like Margaret Mead extolled its uniqueness. It received much publicity, and Bali became synonymous with tropical beauty and exotic adventure.

As foreign administrators, traders, and finally tourist promoters, moved into the island, the process of social change took its inevitable toll.

A curious little picture can be drawn around the custom of dress. In traditional Balinese society, women were always naked from the waist upward but the whole of the lower half of their body was covered by a full-length sarong. When the Europeans began to arrive, a combination of puritanism and uncertainty resulted in social pressures which led the women of the island to cover their breasts with a blouse. One of the cultural niceties which was completely unknown to visiting foreigners was that Balinese men had rarely seen a woman's ankle or the lower part of the leg, because of the long sarong. The short dress of the visitors was offensive to the Balinese women and stimulating to the local men. Just as Western young men find bare breasts titillating, so the Balinese young men find excitement in the forbidden sight of women's ankles. On the Balinese roads you see Western young men on motor-bikes travelling to the remote villages to watch the beautiful Balinese women's upper torso and passing Balinese young men driving their bikes down from the hills to sit at the beach and watch the young Western women's lower torso.

In this little story we have a capsule of the cultural contradictions which tourism produces. When there is an overt clash of value systems and moral beliefs, something has to change. In this case — as in so many others — it is the host community which must adapt its own customs to fit the preconceptions of the visitors.

There are well-founded fears that Balinese culture will change in unforeseen ways which will not improve the quality of life or build up the positive aspects of local culture. At the Udayana University of Denpasar, the island's capital, researchers completed in 1974 a comprehensive report on tourism's impact on Bali's employment, art forms and general way of life.[1] It spoke of dramatic changes in social and cultural patterns. Religious ceremonies, religious dance, gamelan music and traditional crafts were all being changed and subverted to fit the tastes of the tourist. The report gave a long list of examples. Temples had been pillaged for artifacts to sell to the tourists, old customs such as goto-royong (everyone helping everyone else in a community project) were dying out, and commercialism had crept into every aspect of life.

Dr Moerdowo, one of the Udayana researchers, cited an example of the cultural implications.[2] A famous dance in Bali, the kechak dance, was sometimes performed for special village occasions and, since one of the results of the dance was that participants entered a trance, the whole enactment would take several hours. In recent years the tourist choreographers have begun to stage-manage the dance and have reduced it in time to about 15 minutes. The religious nuances of the dance are gone, and it continues to develop more variations to cater to the short attention-span of the tourist. There are some interesting economic injustices in this whole activity. The dance requires a large group of people and the tour operators have to negotiate with a whole village in order to obtain a sufficient number of participants. A study made in 1975 showed that the price paid to the village would be about $20, and since there were up to 200 dancers participating in the dance, it works out at a payment of 10 cents per person. The tour operator collects an average of $250 as entrance fees from the tourists. These figures are a simple but dramatic confirmation of the exploitation which we have already dealt with.

When the Udayana report was first released, government officials voiced concern about its implications for the future of Bali. There was some talk, but little action. Indeed it was about the same time that the developers began to unveil their new plan to create a whole new tourism area in Nusa Dua which would provide 6,950 new beds by 1985. When the agreement was signed, the cultural implications were hardly mentioned.

The Udayana report was published when there were only 85,000 visitors to Bali per year. In 1980 the number of visitors exceeded 500,000 and the forecasts are for continued increases.

At what stage will it become too late to save some aspects of Balinese culture? In October 1980, Indonesia's Communication Minister, Air Marshal Rusmin Nuryadin, warned that "coming generations might have to pay a heavy price for the foreign currency we are getting from tourism." His address at a tourism seminar in Jakarta gave rise to a fresh wave of concern in the public media over the effects of tourism on Bali.[3]

A leading Hindu priest regretted that "now the usually devoted Balinese hold cremations specially for tourists." He claimed that Balinese culture and traditions are threatened by such actions as the selling of worthless marriage licences to foreigners and the corruption of traditional religious ceremonies. Another Balinese noted that the "young men are corrupted. They don't care so much to work, and they prefer to hang around with foreigners or make a living out of short-time romances with fair-haired girls."

A significant part of Bali's tourism is of the 'hippie' type. These young alternative tourists become addicted to Bali's beauty and easy-going lifestyle and remain in the area for months at a time. Many come from neighbouring Australia and New Zealand but the numbers from Europe are also increasing. I have met several young people from Australia who work for a few months in their own country and earn enough money to live in Bali for a year or more. In the underground of the alternative tourist, Bali is a cheap area to live. For $100 per month or less one can live in some comfort in a room rented from local people. The local police officer at Kuta looks at the scene with helpless resignation. According to him "the young people think it is legal to smoke marijuana, go around naked, eat hallucinogenic mushrooms and get drunk."

There is no accurate way to measure how much this semi-permanent pleasure-seeking population has affected Kuta, but one indicator frequently mentioned by the local residents is that until 15 years ago crimes of violence and theft were completely unknown in that area. Residents can actually point to the first murder in Kuta. Now there are many brutal and senseless killings each year, and cases of theft have become so common that security guards and electronic devices have entered the region for the first time.

Bali is an important illustration of the theme we are considering. A poor and overpopulated section of a much larger but still underdeveloped nation, it is limited in its economic potential to develop. Tourism was seen by many leaders in Bali as a solution to the economic depression. When we look at the large hotels, improved roads and airport, and the number of people who work in the tourist industry we seem to see clear signs of economic growth. But there are qualifications. Most of the economic gain in real terms goes overseas or to Jakarta. It does not help Bali, and the actual improvement in the villagers' standard of living is

negligible. Nor does tourism contribute anything in human terms. How do we talk about human development in a place where the culture of the people is being challenged at every point by a powerful counter-culture backed with financial and technological resources which drown the little voices of the village people?

Islands like Bali are particularly vulnerable. Another area whose problems have been well documented is Hawaii. The profound changes taking place in that island as a result of tourism have resulted in a bitter and angry local population.[4]

Native Hawaiians were almost swept aside a century ago, but in recent years they have returned in strength and now dominate the under 20-year population of the islands. To a great extent they remain a society apart from the Caucasian and Japanese mainstream, unassimilated into the economy, the educational system or the culture. They are aliens in their own land.

On the outskirts of Honolulu, and throughout the parks and beaches of Oahu, native Hawaiians have set up temporary squatters' huts and tents because they can no longer afford even slum quarters. In Hawaiian 'homestead' areas, like the Waianae Coast, tourist buses are regularly showered with debris and cries of 'haole go home!' On the islands of Maui, Molokai, Hawaii and Kauai, the traditional 'aloha spirit' of openness, courtesy and hospitality is turning to suspicion, anger and even hostility.

The indigenous people of Bali and Hawaii perceive an even broader threat in the threat to their culture. They see a society losing its sense of history and of continuity with the past, and opting for a vast undifferentiated international culture founded on money-power and the gratification of the senses. Tourism is seen as eroding ancient values and customs, not all of which may have been beneficial, but all of which, taken together, provided a unique way of life which cannot be replaced. Today the remnants of a proud and ancient culture possessed by the Hawaiians has been bastardized into the image of an overweight tourist trying to do a belly-dance with rows of plastic rain-gods watching silently from the shelves of the souvenir store.

A living culture

A nation's culture is the setting in which human development can take place, or, in some cases, where human development is retarded. At its best it is an environment in which the people can develop their lives creatively with freedom and in justice.

Culture is dynamic. A living culture is always in the process of change. It brings stability and a sense of purpose to community through its continuity with the historic process; at the same time it reflects the present experiences and future aspirations of the people.

When we speak of tourism changing traditional society, it is important to note that we are not opposing change *per se*. What is called in question is the direction of the change, the way in which it takes place and why the change happens. There is a significant difference between a change that takes place within the dynamic of the society itself and by decision of that society and a change that is imposed on a culture by external forces which are not always sympathetic to the society.

If we narrow our consideration to a single aspect of cultural development, the anxiety can be better understood. The artist is on the frontier of every society. In traditional culture, the artist receives high recognition and respect. Whether the artist works in wood, ochres, bark, metal or plants, the skill and vision of the artist speak to the members of that culture in a unique way.

When seen from the outside, a particular form of art may appear to be quite static and unimaginative, because the differences in the work are too subtle for outsiders to understand. What seems to be an ordinary work of art can sometimes be a powerful social commentary. In other words, there is creativity and change taking place within the discipline of that art form.

What happens to the artist when the visitor arrives? The protagonists of tourism will claim that at last the artist's gifts are recognized (in monetary terms) and that the art of the community is being encouraged. They will point to the fact that many people can obtain employment and that dying arts are now being revived. In fact the art that is being produced changes in a dramatic way when the tourist comes. The artist finds he (it is usually 'he') is going through four stages.

First, he soon discovers that the new arrivals are ignorant of the meaning of most of his art. They may like the colours or form but the living significance is not understood. Mistakes are not perceived, and thus the standard of the art work drops when the artist learns that he can get away with anything.

The next discovery is that the tastes of the tourist differ from his own. Certain colour combinations are more acceptable. He discovers that size and weight are important because the tourist prefers small carvings and paintings which can be carried easily. It is inconvenient to take back by plane large frames. The art changes in the direction of the market.

Next he will find to his surprise that there is a conservatism in the tourist which prevents him from developing the art in new directions. He can go in one direction, but not another. In the home of a Balinese artist who is trying to develop new forms of art which will speak to his people about social concerns, a German art dealer was heard saying: "Yes, I agree, it is very good, but it will not sell because it is not Balinese." The concept of what makes an art work 'real Balinese' is defined by the tourist and the foreigner rather than by the Balinese artists and the Balinese people.

In the final stage, the artist finds himself taken over by technology and inferior artists. In the village of Paete in the Philippines, which has been a wood-carving centre for centuries, the chip of the chisel has been drowned out by the whir of electric saws, lathes and routers. 'Genuine' Hawaiian wood-carvings are produced in thousands on these machines and shipped to Honolulu. The demand for mass-produced tourist souvenirs overtakes and outprices the painstaking craftspeople, and the art of centuries in Paete is reduced to pathetic carvings of naked women on bottle openers or crude carvings of men in a barrel.

The struggle for artistic integrity is real for all indigenous artists. We had a striking example of this in Guatemala. The tribal Indian people, who comprise 54% of the population of that country, revolted against the prostitution of their dance forms for the tourists, and their reaction became an international incident when the International Food and Allied Workers Union met in June 1980 and demanded an international boycott of tourism to Guatemala because of the exploitation of the Indians.

> The local Indians are angry at the way their culture is being commercialized and thus perverted. The rituals on the steps of Sto Thomas used to be reserved for special occasions because of their meaning. Now the national tourist board pays poor people to perform these rites every Thursday and Sunday when the tourists come to the outdoor market. A meeting of the Indian queens takes place at Coban once a year. The tourist board turned this into a tourist attraction and charged an entrance fee (thus excluding the local population). The young women refused to participate. The Guatemalan government forced the young women to go to Coban by threatening them and their families.

The Generals who run things in rural areas made a good profit from the festival by charging $15 per head from spectators.[5]

Not only were the Indians cheated but the tourists were treated to a ceremony which was not genuine. Angry Indians objected that ''now they want to cheat us again by putting on folkloric festivals in order to give away ridiculous medals, diplomas, false friendliness and sweet smiles to the few Indians on exhibit. We Indians get the least of the benefits of tourism.''

Experiences such as these are commonplace for indigenous people around the world who become exhibits in a tourist zoo. Tourist dollars do not help develop the art of the people; the art actually degenerates and loses its importance to the community.

The loss of a heritage

With the Western recognition of the riches of the culture of developing nations, there came a new threat. Museums, private collections and rich individuals began to covet the irreplaceable historic treasures of the poor countries.

The plundering of a national heritage is not caused by tourism. It was carried out for centuries by colonial rulers, but in recent years the process has accelerated, helped by the tourist phenomenon. The problem of the thief is to find a safe buyer and, with the large number of foreigners, all seeking to find a real bargain, there is a much increased market for illegal goods.

In 1966, Thailand made a magnificent archeological discovery in Ban Chiang which pointed to a civilization dating back over 5,000 years. Within a month unscrupulous dealers were paying undercover prices for anything that looked like an old pot from a funeral mound. Villagers were happy to sell whatever they could, and thousands became involved in a lucrative trade, and artifacts were shipped out of the country in alarming numbers.

Several countries, including Thailand, now have laws which prohibit tourists from taking artifacts out of the country without a permit. This has however not been quite successful in suppressing the trade. The headless Buddhas of Indonesia and the Sri Lankan temples without the old scrolls speak for the continuing desecration and the continuing demand for souvenirs.

A recent series of advertisements to sponsor a new African destination for tourism ran publicity under the slogan: "Go there while it is still unspoiled." Many people would fail to see the irony in such a phrase. The very industry which promotes tourism is aware of the fact that what it promotes is a process of spoiling the naturalness of the place. The arrival of the tourist will challenge and possibly even destroy the culture they are seen as promoting.

The uniqueness of a nation's culture is expressed in its song and art, in its dance and architecture. It is these which draw the tourists to a new country in the first place. It is a sad irony that the culture which attracts the tourist is the thing their presence will destroy. This is expressed by the American song-writer Joni Mitchell who visited Hawaii and wrote the popular song 'Big Yellow Taxi':

> They paved paradise
> And they put up a parking lot
> With a pink hotel, a boutique
> And a swinging hot-spot.
> Don't it always seem to go
> That you don't know what you got
> Till it's gone?

When church leaders from the third world met for a tourism consultation in the Philippines, they reserved their hardest words for what one paper termed 'the bastardization of culture'.[6] A bastard is a child born of an illicit relationship. The bastard does not belong fully to either parent. Out of tourism is born a bastard culture, and one parent leaves without accepting any responsibility for the child left behind.

V. Prostitution tourism

Go into the lobby of one of a number of Philippine hotels, and you will see clusters of Japanese tourists. The Japanese comprise the largest number of visitors to the friendly islands of the Philippines, and special concessions are granted to ensure that the numbers do not decrease.

If you leave the lobby of the hotel and walk around the back to the service entrance of the hotel towards dusk, you will see an extraordinary sight. Rows of taxis, cars and mini-buses pull in out of sight of the road, and a long procession of beautiful young Philippine girls will slip past the guards and into a private entrance of the hotel. You follow them, and you find that they sign a book, hand over their I.D. card and then enter a private elevator to an upper floor. The room each girl will go to is on one of the special floors designated for Japanese prostitution only. The girl knows in advance which room is hers, and if the occupant of that room is out shopping or otherwise engaged, she will just sit in the corridor and wait.

Because of the way in which some floors are isolated in the hotel, it is possible for guests to stay for days and be completely unaware of what is taking place. They will not know that in some of the larger hotels upwards of 500 girls will enter on holidays; between 300 and 400 on ordinary nights. Before breakfast the next morning the girls collect their I.D. cards and leave the hotel as surreptitiously as they arrived.

The Japanese customer had arranged for his tryst with a prostitute even before he left Tokyo. In some cases he has selected the girl from a book of photographs. He has paid the travel agent the sum of $50. From this money, the tour operator has paid a few middle-men. The pimp in Manila gets $20. The average payment to the girl is $8. Once in Manila the Japanese guest pays an additional $12 to the hotel for having the extra person in his room.

To the hotel it is a simple source of extra, and probably tax-free money. The real money is made by the pimps. In Manila, as in many third world cities, the control of the trade is in the hands of the police and the military. When you speak with the girls, they will sometimes reveal that the person who employs them is a high-ranking officer in the military or even the secret service.

The pimps control the trade and make the money. The fee they take from the Japanese tour operator is only a part of their income. They own many large central apartment blocks which are leased to the prostitutes at exorbitant amounts. The girls live six or more to a room. They are forced to remain there because if they try to find separate accommodation, they will not be able to get work in the hotels.

The hotel employs the largest number of girls. Most of the girls are young. Their lot is a hard one. Some of them take such a battering that they have to retire at an early age. Japanese guests generally do not speak the local languages and their brief relationship with the girl is solely physical — sometimes violent. In one of the more notorious hotels in Manila — one which gets the largest number of Japanese tourists — the management has been forced to stop all women from servicing the rooms of tourists. Girls who served as chambermaids or servants were constantly being molested and at least two had been forcibly raped.

If you speak to the girl in confidence, you will soon discover how much she has been victimized. She has become a prisoner of circumstances, and if there were a simple and honest way out she would quickly take it. Now she lives in a fantasy world. She dreams that one day a rich man will come and take her away from this prison.

Almost all the girls have come from the provinces, lured by the promise of work and wealth in the big city. They arrive, innocent and trusting, at one of the central bus depots, and are easy prey for the ladies whose job is to recruit new girls. They are older women who speak several local dialects and who have cultivated a kindly manner to gain the girls' confidence.

The girls from the country are identified by their nervousness. They are delighted to find such a kindly old woman taking an interest in their plight. The helpful lady takes the young girl to her own home and encourages her to look for work. Of course no work is available to a girl from the country, and as the days pass, her debt to the old lady grows. Gradually the girl is initiated into the only solution. If she resists seduction, she will be raped. In either case the 'virgin fee' which the old lady gets will be considerable. The girl is placed in increasing bondage, sold to a pimp and kept in a kind of neo-slavery. Often she is kept off contraceptives, and she becomes pregnant before she starts on her new career. In this way her slavery is confirmed. Plagued with guilt at having an illegitimate child, she now has to put aside all scruples and work at whatever is offered so that she can pay for the care and education of her child.

Social workers estimate that there are now 50,000 prostitutes in Manila alone. While most of the girls work the hotels or hang out in bars, some graduate in the prostitution hierarchy. There are a number of private houses which cater exclusively for Japanese tourists. In this case, the tourist bus travels around the sights of the city and at some stage calls in at the private house by a back door. The group troops into the building and are told they have one hour. Behind closed doors and windows they choose a girl. An hour later, as the bell rings, they march out to the bus and continue their tour of the city.

At the top of the prostitution hierarchy are the few select girls who are the hostesses in the private clubs. These cater mostly for the very wealthy Japanese or Americans. The cover charge will be around $100 and this gives an evening in plush and discreet surroundings. Each drink and extra service from the girls will add to the bill, so by the end of the night several hundred dollars have changed hands.

Once a city gets the reputation of being a centre for sexual gratification it has to follow all the trends. It must now cater to varieties of homosexual and heterosexual experiences. It must provide for sexual perversions. In Manila, as in other similar centres, the growth of child prostitution is alarming. In this case, the pimps visit the poor rural areas and negotiate to buy children or lease them for about $50 per year. Young children, both girls and boys from the age of about 8, are taught to perform sexual acts for voyeurs and later are placed in brothels which cater for paedophiliacs.

Such wide and pervasive prostitution cannot take place without positive official connivance. In third world countries the police and military are involved, but increasingly in recent years the action groups have secured evidence of the involvement of highly placed politicians and government officers. Although the politicians always decry the development of prostitution their words carry little credibility.

When men live or travel on their own, separated from families, they are set free from the normal moral restraints which exist at home. It is understandable then that the origins of the present wide trade in prostitution in Asia can be traced to the presence of foreign military bases in the continent.

Prior to 1955, prostitution in Asia was less pervasive, and either followed the local customs or flourished around the major ports. This changed with the establishment of major military bases in Asia and it reached its peak during the war in Vietnam. At this time, tens of thousands of healthy young men were caught up in a war which they didn't understand and which failed to capture their hearts and minds. To maintain morale, the forces resorted to a programme called rest and recreation, which financed the travel of these thousands of young men to nearby centres to get away from the fighting. Each six months they had a month's leave and the descent of thousands of free-spending affluent American soldiers was a lure to local entrepreneurs, who established whole new streets of vice overnight. In Bangkok, Taipei, Hong Kong and Manila the demand for girls was insatiable.

The development of the massage parlour dates from this time. Massage has a long and honourable history in many parts of Asia and is still respected in many cultures. The business interests now took up massage and turned it into a front for prostitution.

At the end of the Vietnam war, massage parlours with their related bars and brothels had a brief period of inactivity, but the American soldiers were soon replaced by the West European and Japanese tourists. The massage parlours now became more gaudy. Customers could enter a comfortable lounge and, while they sipped their beer, could watch through a one-way mirror large numbers of girls sitting and talking together. If one of the girls appeared attractive to the customer he would arrive at a price, and take the girl to a private room.

The customer identified the girl by a number which was hung around her neck. The girl was not given a name; she became simply a number in the circle. The reduction of people to digits is not uncommon in this kind of dehumanizing relationship. There is an ultimate impersonality in being known simply as 'number 47' in a hall of 150 girls.

As this phenomenon grew throughout Asia, a few student and women's groups began to organize themselves against it. In 1973 the first demonstration took place in Kimpo airport in Seoul, Korea, where students from Ewha Women's University held banners which said: "Our motherland should not be turned into a brothel for Japanese men." Japanese action groups responded, and soon there was a vigorous campaign in many other parts of Asia.

In January 1981, Prime Minister Suzuki of Japan travelled through Southeast Asia and was surprised to be confronted with strong protest groups attacking Japanese sex tourism in both Manila and Thailand. A protest letter prepared by 68 organizations in the Philippines said: "We would like to forget Japanese military imperialism. But now instead of military uniforms, the men come in business suits dominating Asia through a pernicious form of socio-economic imperialism which tramples on the Asian peoples' right to human dignity."[1]

Commenting on this letter the Moderator of the Church of Christ in Japan observed that "prostitution tourism is not only a question of individual sexual ethics, but it has to be seen more deeply in its relation to the social structures of today."[2]

Within this perspective we are able to see the reality of the exploitation which is taking place. It is the economic imbalance between the relatively wealthy tourist and the shocking poverty of the poor people in the farms and slums which makes prostitution flourish in third world countries. As the writer Takasato Suzuyo points out about Japanese tourism, "sexual exploitation must be seen as one part of the larger economic exploitation which characterizes Japan's relations with other countries."[3]

If governments had the will they could effectively put down such organized prostitution. Nor has every third world country depended on prostitution to develop a tourist industry. The development of tourism without prostitution may be a slower road but at least it is one which third world countries could take with more dignity.

VI. The politics of tourism

There is an enormous gap between the tourist publicity description of a country and the actual social and political reality. The men and women who are employed to sell a country through publicity are in the business of selling illusions. The brochures about some of the well-known tourist destinations make interesting reading. Poor third world countries are described in theological language as 'heaven' and 'paradise.' Islands become 'pearls'; they are 'bewitching', 'exotic', 'enchanting', 'excitingly primitive'.

This is the myth of tourism. The truth about many of these places is that half the population live in abject poverty; large numbers of people are illiterate, unemployed and poorly housed, with a life-expectancy much shorter than that of the tourists.

It is one of the axioms of tourist publicity that you tell only the good side. No advertisement will warn the tourists that they will be "surrounded by beggars, many of whom will not earn in a lifetime what the tourist spends on a single trip." The publicity will not say that in some places foreigners are so unwelcome that their buses will be stoned and that many tourists are physically assaulted every year.

Tourism is sold through the myth that the sun always shines, the natives always smile and they are so friendly that the tourist can walk anywhere in perfect safety.

This indeed is the ultimate service industry. Tourism, particularly in third world countries, instils a form of mass servility. The island of Jamaica is passing through a period of massive social upheaval, and the government is attempting to use tourism as a force for change. In an advertising campaign on USA television, they depict a game of polo which includes one shot of a black man playing polo. This totally alien stereotype is accompanied by the words: "Come back to gentility — come back to Jamaica." The image of life as it used to be is the myth which tourism advertising promotes.

Since this is what tourism offers and demands, it is not surprising that dictators in every oppressed society are falling over themselves to turn their country into a tourist resort. No country lives to itself and even the most secure tyrant has to worry about his international image. He must have a good image so that he can, among other things, develop his country's economy and secure foreign aid and assistance.

Tourism comes into this situation like a Cinderella's wand. It feeds on dreams. No matter what the internal costs, many rulers rush eagerly into tourism to bolster their national image in the eyes of the world.

Some countries are quite open about this policy. The International Workshop on Tourism heard from Philippine Government Tourism officials who openly stated that President Marcos had a bad image in the Western press because of his programme of martial law, and tourism provided an opportunity to change this image. In an action unprecedented in recent years, the Philippine government had laid out more than $300 million of its own cash to subsidize the building of fourteen luxury hotels along the Manila waterfront. This was rushed through in time for the meeting of the World Bank and International Monetary Fund in 1976. Generous tax concessions and financial assistance encouraged chains such as Holiday Inn, Western Hotels, Ramada Inn and Sheraton to establish hotels in the country.

The building boom gave Manila the largest line of five-star hotels in Asia, but occupancy has been so low that few are making any profit. Of the eight major hotels which have filed returns for 1980, only three made any profit, while some recorded losses in excess of 3 million dollars. Occupancy has climbed painfully from only 40% in 1977 to 69% in 1980, but this was achieved by offering cut prices, and the result is that many hotels have defaulted on payments and become the property of the Central Bank.[1]

None of this deterred the ambitious plans of President Marcos and his energetic First Lady. They have projects to develop beaches to entice the 'Cannes' film festival to Manila and will expend vast sums of money to encourage international conferences to meet in Manila. As expenditure on tourism reaches new heights, the expenditure on improving the conditions of the poor sections of the community goes down. When $300 million was spent in 1976 to build five-star hotels, less than $15 million was spent on housing and public buildings.

Since there appears to be little economic profit in the exercise, the rationale behind the tourist development is clearly political. The Philippine leadership reasoned that if a sufficient number of Western people, especially opinion-makers, were to visit the Philippines and enjoy the experience, they would counteract the negative voices of those who spoke about gross denials of human rights in the country. In this giant public relations exercise, the greatest supporters were the tireless copywriters of advertisements: "Since President Marcos imposed martial law... the tourism industry has undergone a great change. It has become purposeful. It has received government support." Martial law is described as 'benevolent' and the writer concludes, "trees have been planted everywhere and private armies have been abolished."[2]

In every continent, there are examples of how tourism has been adopted to fit the image of an oppressive ruler. In the Caribbean, Haiti has for some years been recognized as one of the more repressive states. Although it became the first independent black nation in the world, its subsequent history has been one of brutality and human rights violations. In the 1970's, repression under the infamous 'Papa Doc' Duvalier reached new heights. The country slid further into economic stagnation, with 90% of the five million people on the island illiterate and 50% close to starvation.

The Duvalier family lived a life of luxury in the midst of all this, in part because they could lease the most attractive sections of the coast line to tourist groups. The most ostentatious example of this was Habitation Leclerc.[3] This extravagant hotel is described as one of the five most affluent hotels in the world and will cost the guest more than $200 per night, slightly more than what the average Haitian will earn in two years. The "most extraordinarily lascivious and decadent place on earth", that was how the promoter of the hotel, Olivier Coquelin of New York, described it.

Papa Doc, Haiti's ruler for life, has since died and been succeeded by his son Jean Claude who has vowed to replace terrorism with tourism. He has hidden the outward signs of his father's reign of terror, but for the country's inhabitants little has changed. They are still reluctant to talk politics with strangers, and most continue poor, proud and hungry.

Tourism helps to sustain the dictatorships of the right. The tourists who are attracted to such countries represent the success stories of right-wing capitalist economies. They reflect a system which enables a large section of the population to accumulate wealth in excess of needs, and to spend it unthinkingly in the course of a leisure holiday. In many among the host population, this lifestyle creates envy and expectation. The tourist gives the poor a substitute dream.

TOM AND I TRAVELLED THROUGH TEN EUROPEAN COUNTRIES AND FIVE IN AFRICA BUT IT WASN'T VERY INTERESTING

But tourism can also be made use of by the politics of the left. Many of the concerned spectators from the host country regard the tourists as over-indulged bourgeoise and as enemies of the poor. This was the case in Cuba. When local feelings run high, tourism itself becomes one of the mechanisms of change. Fidel Castro channelled the anger of the local people and used it effectively in his struggle.

With the growth of a leisure class in Eastern Europe, tourism has spread to communist countries. Resorts near the inland seas of Eastern Europe now rival those on the Mediterranean. Since Western observers seldom get the chance to visit these resorts, little reliable information is available on tourism in these countries. It can, however, be assumed from the way it is often described, that it plays a role in placating and domesticating the middle-classes in communist states.

The other major communist country to embrace tourism is the People's Republic of China. Until 1978, tourism was seen by China as a form of propaganda. The number of tourists was limited. Those who took the package tour were exposed to a remarkable variety of daily experiences. Tourists would visit rural communes, hospitals, factories, housing settlements and schools. With greatly increased numbers of tourists travelling to China the programme is now being geared to more scenic tourism, but the political overtones are still evident in the way in which the country is interpreted to visitors.

In the politics of both capitalism and communism, tourism is used as a means of muffling opposition and domesticating discontent. As the myth is created that the economy depends on tourism, people are pressured into doing nothing to upset the tourist. This is especially true of the scattered island states where the population is small enough to be controlled. The French made good use of the technique in the Pacific, and deluged Tahiti and New Caledonia with so many tourists and visitors that the forces in the islands working for change were for a time muzzled.

The small island of Singapore has become Asia's largest single destination for tourists. It is an excellent illustration of a society which has changed its cultural and social patterns in order to conform to tourism expectations. Although the 'economic miracle' of Singapore does not depend solely (or even primarily) on tourism, it is still important enough to be used to reinforce the domesticating policies of the government.

A continual stream of slogans exhort the population to obey one or another of the local laws, and once a year there is a 'Courtesy Campaign' in which a whole series of rewards and punishments encourages the people to smile, and be amiable and helpful. Prime Minister Lee says it will take ten years for the lesson to sink in. While courtesy is an admirable virtue, its linkage with the country's tourism drive is a further step towards a controlled society.

Tourism, like all other social and economic activities, must be subjected to the questioning which will have as its focus the well-being of the whole population. For this reason the International Workshop on Tourism spoke of finding alternative forms of tourism:

> It is a requirement that we find ways to return tourism to the people so that the experience of travel will enrich all. By returning the tourism industry to the people, the economic benefits can be more fully shared, and the people can participate fully in decision-making.[4]

VII. Can tourism be salvaged?

When representatives of the Ecumenical Coalition on Third World Tourism met officials of the World Tourism Organisation in Madrid, Spain, to report on the church consultation, the WTO claimed that the emphasis of the churches was biased, and the churches focused on the negative side of tourism. Insofar as the churches reflect the voices of ordinary third world people who are concerned for human development, the churches are right to sound the negative note.

This always comes as a surprise to many Western people. Over the years we have been conditioned to see tourism in positive terms, and the massive publicity machinery of the tourism industry has done its best to reinforce that impression. Tourism has so often been commended as making a healthy and positive contribution to the world's economy and to peace and friendship among nations. Most tourists will echo such sentiments.

It is hard for people living in affluent societies to understand the gap between this view and that of articulate Christians in third world countries who will assert that tourism "wreaks more havoc than benefit", as the Manila tourism conference stated.

In attacking tourism as it is practised today, the third world is not being inhospitable. That would be unthinkable in a traditional society where the guest must be given the best of everything, and treated with courtesy and respect. But tourists are no longer guests. They arrive without being invited by the local people, they establish an impersonal contractual relationship with the host businesses, and they pay their own way.

Nevertheless, in spite of all that we have said, it is still important to ask the question which came from the Manila conference: "Can tourism be salvaged?"

Most of the criticism of tourism is directed at the resort-centred tourism, which caters for large numbers of individual group or charter travellers. Since this is the largest and potentially the most destructive form of tourism, it needs to be approached with some caution by third world countries. We offer three general comments:

1. Resort tourism must be preceded by an educational programme, and the people who are affected must share in the discussion and decisions concerning tourism development.

This is a minimal requirement if we are speaking of human development. In too many nations (and not only in the third world), decisions are made by rulers and then foisted on the people. This will inevitably increase the alienation of the people from the programme and create social tension. The unilateral action of Papa Doc Duvalier in Haiti, who sold off the beautiful Haitian sea coast without reference to any of the local people, is the worst example of a leader ignoring the interests of the local people.

Compare this with what happens in the island of BoraBora in the Pacific.[1] The church there is so strong that before any action is taken in areas of tourism, whether it be the construction of new buildings or initiating some action which will affect local customs, the Council of Deacons from the church sits down to negotiate a mutually acceptable solution with the hotel management. Such negotiation ends with a solution which the people will understand and which will not offend local custom.

Much of the initial misunderstanding begins with the selection of a site for a resort. In third world countries there are indeed beautiful locations which can be developed as resorts without antagonizing the local people. Unfortunately it is more common to ignore these places in favour of immediately accessible sites, regardless of their past and present associations with the life and religion of the people. A respect for the cultural and religious importance of the land must be shared by all parties. It is these traditional values attached to land and sites which have maintained the fabric of the whole race in the past. To bulldoze traditional ways in the name of economic progress is to ignore and destroy the values which make that society unique to the visitor.

The architectural forms which cater to tourism must be acceptable to the people. The hotel industry often imposes foreign models on a poor country, which clash violently with local architecture. The economical high-rise hotel, which is rather like an over-grown battery-hen operation, is the favourite choice.

When the first of these concrete boxes was erected on the island of Bali, the people were outraged and let their anger be known so loudly that the local government hastily passed a new law that future hotels should be no taller than a coconut tree. Forced to look at new models, hotel planners discovered that local building styles were indeed suitable for their needs and some impressive small hotels which harmonize with the environment have subsequently been built along the shore.

The cultural imperialism of hotels can be avoided by working with the people. Conrad Hilton would probably never understand this. In one of his heavy quotes, he stated that "each of our hotels is a little America." What is the point of travelling half-way round the planet to stay in a hotel which is the same as the one down your street? But Hilton, the representative hotel owner, has other motivations, as he stated in his autobiography: "I sincerely believe we are doing our bit to spread world peace, and to fight socialism."[2]

If the people are involved in each step of tourism development the dislocation to society will be minimized, though the development will be slower. To those who are seeking quick profit, this may be tiresome, but it will pay long-term dividends. The economic benefit to the local people will also be increased, as tourism will then protect local interests and encourage the practice of local crafts.

2. The tourism resort should be kept separate from the daily life of the people.

The development of tourist enclaves has been opposed by many developers but it makes a lot of sense in third world countries. By confining the tourist to a relatively small area of the country the impact on the local population will be kept to a minimum. This means that tourist resorts should be self-sufficient, geographically isolated, and must have facilities and attractions which will keep the tourist within the resort area.

By using indigenous styles, artists and food, the illusion of being a part of a foreign community can be sustained.

Just as Disneyworld and Disneyland can create environments, so should the tourist-receiving country establish its own miniature worlds for the sake of the mass tourist.

Thailand has created some mini-Thailands. One called 'Thailand in Miniature' (TIM) offers samples of the country in a small park. Here the tourist can see elephants working, peasants planting rice, irrigation machinery made of bamboo, traditional houses and similar attractions. In another centre, 'The Ancient City', many old and unused temples have been taken from the provinces and rebuilt or reproduced in a single area which can be covered in a day, and gives an excellent background to Buddhism and its architecture.

Such enclaves will help to preserve the on-going life of the country and avoid all the countless embarrassing incidents which occur when tourists climb unthinkingly over sacred sites or disrupt social patterns through their dress and habits.

A few other countries have already taken small steps towards this separation. An increasing number of ethnic ar-

tists and cultural performers are taking their crafts and skills to the hotels rather than have bus-loads of foreigners descend on their village. This helps restore dance and music to their proper perspective. It becomes now a performance for foreigners, and the basic religious intent of the dance and music can be reserved for the normal performance in the temples or the village centre.

The tourists generally have only a superficial interest in the culture of the country. They will enjoy something a little different and colourful, but will be just as happy to pop their flash lights in the hotel beside the pool as in a dusty village square.

The flow of tourist buses through local villages and peasant areas often becomes an unpardonable invasion of privacy. Traditional societies are resentful when someone takes photos of them without permission. In some Asian places it is seen as stealing a part of their psyche. Call to mind the familiar picture of the tourists leaning out of the windows of their bus to take photos with a tele-lens of women bathing in a river or villagers cooking their meal on a fire. Then picture for ourselves the reversal of this process. Imagine a group of foreign people, wearing strange clothes, speaking none of the local languages, trespassing into the gardens of a house in London, New York, Sydney or Stuttgart, peering through the windows, and taking photos with tele-lens of the husband washing the dishes or the wife in the bath. In Western society, people would be shocked and scandalized and would call the police. Yet this is precisely what tourists in the third world are doing day after day.

The solution to many of the difficulties of mass tourism is to confine the tourist movement as much as possible. Move them rapidly from the airport to a tourism enclave; create the illusion of exotica; ban all surface travel outside a restricted area, and then at the end of the time whisk them off and on to the plane to the next fantasyland.

In fact this may be what the tourists want. In coming to the country they have already been seduced by a land that doesn't exist. Now give them the beautiful dream world of the posters, and not the slums and poverty of the cities or the toil and sweat of the villages.

3. Let the tourist pay. Let the people receive.

Finally, the cost structure of tourism must be revised, so that the real income from the tourist should go to the people and the country rather than be siphoned off in franchise payments and repatriated profit. Just as the Organization of Petroleum Exporting Countries created a coalition of oil states for their own protection, third world countries could create a coalition to develop tourism in a way which is at once more human and more profitable for the countries themselves.

It can be argued that many third world countries would be in a much stronger position if they cut down the number of tourists coming to their country and controlled the tourism industry through their own local companies. A number of third world countries now have their own airlines and can create the infrastructure which would enable them to develop tourism their own way. That will take them out of the absurd situation where they are actually providing subsidized holidays for the wealthy foreigner.

The options before third world countries are limited, but with the phenomenal growth of tourism, many of them are reaching the point where there must be some conscious control over the form of the tourist industry, as otherwise the whole society will have to adopt tourism as a way of life and restructure itself to serve the tourist. This would effectively put the control of the state in the hands of a foreign industry which can determine its history in ways similar to those of earlier colonial rulers. Some smaller states in the Caribbean may already have passed the point of no return in this respect.

Eventually, there could well be a tourist tax levied by third world countries. Just as people pay for the use of the airport and the hotel, so there is a case for paying for the use of a country. Such taxation could only be justified if there emerged a mechanism which would enable the money to be used to humanize the tourist encounter with local people. There has been some discussion that possibly an international agency might be formed to administer such a tax for the good of the people.

We have been concentrating here on mass tourism. It is the hardest to organize and control, and it is in the interest of third world governments and agencies to find ways to use such tourism for full human development.

VIII. The other tourists

Why do people take to tourism? So far we have been dealing with the excesses of those who pursue sun, sand and sex. There are many, however, who are not travelling solely in pursuit of pleasure.

The classification of 'types of tourists' has been attempted by several writers. There is little point in repeating what they have said. But there are forms of tourism which we cannot ignore in a study of third world tourism. We shall deal with four of these.

Tourism with a purpose

The educational tour has become popular, not only with students from universities and colleges, but also with specialized groups repesenting vocational, professional or hobby interests. In each case there is a clearly defined area of interest which gives some purpose and focus to the travel.

Normally such groups do not create the kind of confusion which large mass tours cause, but when there is lack of sensitivity on the part of the group, some unfortunate incidents can take place. In February 1974 a tour group from an American school visited Thailand. Six of the students climbed on to a statue of the Buddha which they wanted to photograph. Local people were shocked, and called in the police who arrested the young people. On the following day the students were fined $50 each. The students were all members of a religious group and when the head of this denomination heard the news, he stated that he didn't see why the students should be punished, because they didn't believe in the Buddha and so no sacrilege was committed!

Incidents of such gross insensitivity are fortunately rare. Yet the cultural differences between the host and guest are so great that it is advisable for members of the travelling group to do some real home work before they start on their tour.

Let us make a few general suggestions:

1. The initiative for the visit should come from the local people. Sometimes this is not possible, and the decision to undertake the travel has to be made by the tour group itself. In that case, it is essential that while the tour is still being planned there should be full discussion and participation by

both hosts and guests. It is not sufficient for the tour party to announce the date of arrival and provide a list of its needs. The expectations of both parties must be fully discussed and understood.

2. A large party of visitors can be intimidating to the hosts, and it is unlikely to promote meaningful interaction. Eight to fifteen is a manageable group, and local communities in the third world can handle such a number with comfort.

3. In a third world country, the group should include at least one person who understands local customs and can speak the local language. This person should be responsible for the orientation of the group before the travel begins.

4. Where possible, the group should invite a knowledgeable local person to join them in travelling through the country. In this way, the travellers are helped to see the pressures and hopes of a society through 'a different pair of eyes'. Most real learning will take place en route and local expertise is required to interpret situations and explain customs.

5. The group should stay in one place long enough to gain a real understanding of whatever the members are studying. No educational tour group should give the impression that its members can become experts in a field after a few days of observation and study.

6. It is a good practice for the group to have regular periods of reflection and discussion during their travel, but these should involve the hosts as well. By thus including local people, misconceptions can be removed and new insights gained.

Travel in such specialized groups can be a real learning experience for hosts and guests. Skills can be shared and awareness of new discoveries discussed. Cultures can be compared and contrasted. When undertaken with sensitivity, this is a creative experience for both sides.

The pilgrimage

Travel for the sake of spiritual renewal has a long and venerable history. It is part of the faith of many religions. Each year increasing numbers of travellers visit centres of pilgrimage to seek physical cures, to discharge obligations of faith, and in search of salvation and peace of mind.

One of the five tenets of Islam requires the faithful to make the journey to Mecca at least once in a lifetime. Despite attempts by extremist Moslem groups to use the annual Haj as an occasion for terrorist activities, the number of pilgrims grows and now exceeds one million overseas participants each year.

Buddhism and Hinduism have many centres, with special holy associations in the life of the Buddha, or one of the gods of the Hindu pantheon, or of a Boddhisattva. The point of confluence of the Yamuna and the Ganges in Northern India is a place of annual pilgrimage, and on 19 January 1977 when the great festival of Kumbamela was celebrated, there was a gathering estimated at 12,700,000 persons. The piety which led these devotees to spend months on foot, walking hundreds of miles, makes the pilgrims travelling by jet seem a different species altogether!

Christian pilgrimages were common in medieval Europe but their significance has tended to wane in recent years. Even so, there are particular shrines of Roman Catholicism and Eastern Orthodoxy which continue to attract large numbers of pilgrims every year.

Many tourists are 'curiosity pilgrims'. Lacking the religious faith of earlier years, they visit shrines partly out of curiosity. In addition to established religious centres, secular history has in our time created new shrines for pilgrims. It is not uncommon for visitors to go to such places as Hiroshima or Guadalcanal, or to stand at the grave of Mahatma Gandhi or visit the home of Mao Zedong in China.

At the same time, old shrines have changed from being centres of religious renewal and devotion to become museums. Many of the great cathedrals of Europe must now be placed in this category. A consultation sponsored by the World Council of Churches in May 1975 at Windsor Castle, England, sought ways of speaking some religious word to the millions of visitors who pass through St George's Chapel every year. Although the group which met proposed, and even undertook, some inventive ways to challenge the tourists to think in greater depth of the religious significance of the place they visited, it has not had much impact. It was clear that the tourists, and even some of the people who administered the chapel, were not interested in any attempt to give the chapel a contemporary relevance. It was a relic of past glory, a history lesson in stone, a museum, and most seemed to prefer that it stay that way.

As the old cathedrals are losing their religious significance and becoming tourist attractions, there is a yearning among people to discover new centres of pilgrimage. An important illustration of this is the Protestant community of Taizé in Southern France. Each year this community is deluged with visitors, mostly young people, who participate in the regular worship of the community and create their own structures

of discussion and learning. The church has a great deal to gain from the encouragement of such living centres of pilgrimage.

The pilgrimage has a special place within the religious tradition and we need not assess its significance here. The pilgrim is often single-minded; he or she will not be diverted by other attractions on the journey. The pilgrim's mind-set is different from that of conventional tourists. The pilgrim makes the journey in a spirit of penitence, devotion or gratitude to God, and is likely to be far less demanding of the host culture or of the environment. Much could be accomplished if religious leaders encouraged tourists who leave their shores to travel with a little of the pilgrim mind.

The 'Christian' tour

What we have said about pilgrimages to special shrines should not be confused with a new phenomenon in the world of travel — the 'Christian' tour. A small but thriving new industry has grown up to cater for wealthy Christians of Western countries who shun the self-indulgence of tourism for pleasure, and would rather undertake a 'Christian' tour, preferably with a minister of religion or a priest to lead the way.

Several church-related agencies have begun to adopt this kind of programme. Sometimes it is done in a patronizing way. Participants are invited to travel overseas to see 'their' mission field, 'their' aid project or, with some sponsorship or adoption agencies, 'their' child. While identification with people across national boundaries has its value, such travel under the pretence of extending an understanding of Christian mission has little to commend it.

A key question to be raised is with regard to the source of the initiative. If the Christian community or related organization in a third world country specifically asks for a particular group of foreign visitors, then the matter should be explored, and possibly there may be some real value for the local church in having such a contact. Sometimes a local church needs the encouragement or skills which a particular group of overseas guests can bring to their community. A tour in response to local initiative is, however, rare. More often the idea emerges from conversations in the wealthy country and is welcomed in terms of self-interest. To the leaders, there is the opportunity for cheap or free travel. To the organization, there is the chance to invite some of its wealthy donors to see the projects and, by their becoming more emotionally involved, increase their financial support. When the group returns, they become good salespersons for the organization.

A good many Western aid and mission agencies are organizing church tours to third world countries to look at aid programmes, and the hospitality of the host communities is wearing thin. These people have their own work to do, and the presence of numerous visitors poking around, often asking elementary questions, is a distraction. It is ironical that some of the more successful aid projects in third world countries now find it necessary to employ extra staff simply to take care of foreign visitors. We do not refer to related staff from donor agencies who go to discuss matters of joint action and partnership but to the casual visitors who feel some right of possession, or who are being 'educated' for mission. A sign on one Indian organization notice-board summed it up succinctly: "Please wear your old clothes tomorrow, because another aid group is visiting."

Solidarity tourism

Another form of tour group has emerged in recent years, and it represents an important new development in church relations. It comes from the discovery of many Christian communities in the third world that they desperately need friends of influence in the Western world. Usually this need is felt by those who struggle for human rights in an oppressive situation.

One of the realities of today's world is that many of the decisions which most affect the poor of the third world are actually made in the economic, political and military centres of the large power blocs. Those who struggle for justice in any part of the world need the support of persons in other countries to plead their cause.

One of the experiences of Latin America which has been of help to churches in many countries has been the development of a strategy of learning called 'encuentros'. It seeks to expose people to a living which is new to them, and then to give them a chance to reflect on that situation with their hosts. A new sensitivity and commitment can emerge from such encuentros. The visitors live with the people, sharing their simple food and meagre living standards. They remain long enough to absorb some of the feelings of the people and to empathize with their suffering and hopes.

The initiative for such encounters can come only from the host countries. They are the ones who know the ground well enough to plan the itinerary, and they know the contacts in other countries who have been sympathetic to their situation.

IX. Alternative tourism

One of the significant new facts about tourism is that it is no longer confined to the rich but is available to persons of quite moderate incomes in the Western world. Without understanding any of the dynamics of the country they visit, such tourists are sometimes able to relate to people of another culture in a simple yet effective manner.

Often such tourists are on their first and possibly only leisure trip overseas; they have rarely been in an expensive hotel, and are greatly embarrassed by the ostentation of this lifestyle; they have never had servants and are uncomfortable, through not knowing how to act; they are not academics or persons of great influence in their home country; and they frequently have a genuine interest in other people and a deep compassion towards those in need. Their interest in travel is mainly to meet some other ordinary people and talk about the simple things of life such as bringing up children, employment conditions, gardens and home. They talk softly, and walk humbly.

Local people would like to meet these tourists. By such people they would not feel intimidated. They could talk to them. But unfortunately traditional tourism does not cater for such an experience. It has adopted a particular model which grew out of earlier years when tourists were rich, and expected carpeted hotels, maids to make their rooms and servants to run their errands.

Is it possible to return tourism to the people through alternative models?

It is dangerous to hold up models; they arise out of a particular situation and may not always be transferable. One which has gained international attention and comes nearest to what some of us seek in a more just tourism is the Lower Casamance programme in Senegal, Africa.[1]

The programme started in part as a response to many incidents of conflict in Senegal between tourists and local people. The proud Senegalese reacted strongly against the 'zoo' syndrome so prevalent in the tourism to that country and began to voice violent protest against the forms of tourism being promoted in the region.

Under the sponsorship of the Agency for Cultural and Technical Cooperation, there began a series of discussions with local chiefs and concerned leaders. Anxious to be good hosts but unhappy with the tourist style, the various discussions produced an imaginative programme called 'Tourism for Discovery.' This called for simple lodgings to be built in the style of ordinary village huts. Series of huts were built in the villages themselves and their care and maintenance was assigned to various members of the village. Guests register to stay at the huts and are received as part of the village community. They share in the ordinary life of the people, join in festivities and dance and have ample opportunity to sit and talk with the local people.

A long educational programme preceded the building of the huts, but by 1976 the first programmes were in operation, and the project has continued with modest success ever since. Similar schemes are under way in neighbouring Benin, Mali and Niger.

Christian Saglio, the ethnologist in charge of the programme, remarks: "Surprisingly it is easier for tourists to discover a different way of life and social tradition than it is for the professionals in the field (a reference to travel agents — *ed*.) who remain strongly attached to their own way of doing things."[2]

One value of the Senegal experiment is that it took the people seriously. The whole concept emerged from long and sometimes circular discussions, and still some of these debates continue. But at least the programme belongs to the people and the profits remain in the country.

A further strength is the relatively small capital outlay required to start the programme. The cost is such that almost any third world community could provide the initial facilities.

In some communities alternative programmes for tourists have sprung up spontaneously. The Balinese living in Kuta beach saw the possibilities of setting apart one of the rooms in their house as a room for guests. The charge for this service was astonishingly cheap to the tourist — between $1 and $3 per night and the losman, or house hotel, has become popular with budget tourists. Local people contend that the money which is made by the Balinese community in Kuta is considerably more than the financial benefit which comes to the community from the long line of hotels at Sanur Beach.

Community agencies in third world countries should consider such models as possible ways of assisting the development of their community. While the programme can be open to the same type of abuse as consumer tourism, it is more likely to attract the kind of tourist who will relate to the local community more meaningfully.

The alternative tourist

Since tourism is an exchange of people, we have to return continually to the human factor in discussing the industry. Unlike in other forms of trade, any measurement in terms of profit and loss is misleading and diverts us from the central human encounter.

Stories of the ugly American (or Japanese, German or Australian) are common enough, and we need not go through a recital of all the prejudices, hostility, deceit and dishonesty which are shown by various ethnic groups when they travel in an alien land. But they may well teach us what we should avoid, and they help us picture the kind of constructive behaviour which third world countries have a right to expect from tourists.

In 1975, the Christian Conference of Asia conducted a programme of research on tourism in Asia. Included in the report was a Code of Ethics for travellers.[3] This code has subsequently been translated into several languages and issued as a pamphlet to travellers starting on a journey. Following discussions between representatives of the Australian Council of Churches and the Indonesian airline, Garuda, the airline published a modified version of the Code of Ethics and placed it in the seat pocket of its flights to Indonesia. We give below the text as originally drawn up:

A Code of Ethics for tourists

1. Travel in a spirit of humility and with a genuine desire to learn more about the people of your host country.

2. Be sensitively aware of the feelings of other people, thus preventing what might be offensive behaviour on your part. This applies very much to photography.

3. Cultivate the habit of listening and observing, rather than merely hearing and seeing.

4. Realize that often the people in the country you visit have time concepts and thought patterns different from your own; this does not make them inferior, only different.

5. Instead of looking for that 'beach paradise', discover the enrichment of seeing a different way of life, through other eyes.

6. Acquaint yourself with local customs — people will be happy to help you.

7. Instead of the Western practice of knowing all the answers, cultivate the habit of asking questions.

8. Remember that you are only one of the thousands of tourists visiting this country and do not expect special privileges.

9. If you really want your experience to be 'a home away from home', it is foolish to waste money on travelling.

10. When you are shopping, remember that the 'bargain' you obtained was only possible because of the low wages paid to the maker.

11. Do not make promises to people in your host country unless you are certain you can carry them through.

12. Spend time reflecting on your daily experiences in an attempt to deepen your understanding. It has been said that what enriches you may rob and violate others.

There is nothing particularly 'Christian' in this list; it is basically a collection of commonsense principles. When Garuda Airlines made use of it, they deleted the justice issue in no. 10, and instead carried a useful statement about bargaining which said, among other things: "When you bargain, remember that the poorest merchant would sooner give up his profit than give up his dignity."

If we were rewriting the code today, I would the change the second half of no. 7 to "Cultivate the habit of listening"; Western tourists talk too much, perhaps to cover their own confusion.

Again, photography calls for a stronger warning than we have in no. 2. In many parts of the world there should perhaps be a moratorium on taking photographs of third world people.

A single code of ethics cannot of course speak to every situation, and it is probable that some groups in the third world need to consider again the patterns of behaviour which will be acceptable to them.

Basic human encounter is one of the supreme experiences of life. Tourism has the potential to give that encounter to increased numbers of people. Across the boundaries of nationality and of wealth it should be possible for people to recognize that they belong to one another and are part of a single human family. When tourism realizes its potential for creating that unity, world peace may not be an impossible dream.

NOTES

Chapter 2
1. In the paper presented to the International Consultation on Tourism, Manila, 1980.
2. *Bones and Feathers,* Heinemann, Singapore, 1978.
3. From the magazine *India Today* (date unknown).
4. Turner, L. & Ash, J. *The Golden Hordes,* St Martins Press, New York, 1976, p. 175.
5. Kent, Noel J., *Islands Under the Influence,* unpublished PhD thesis, University of Hawaii, 1979, p. 420.
6. de Kadt, E., *Tourism — Passport to Development,* Unesco-World Bank, Oxford, New York, 1979, p. 67.
7. Turner & Ash, *op. cit,* p. 256.
8. *Asiaweek,* December 1980.

Chapter 3
1. *The Economic, Social and Cultural Impact of Tourism in Sri Lanka,* Christian Worker's Fellowship, Colombo, 1981.
2. *Ibid.*
3. Wood, Robert E., "Tourism and Underdevelopment in South East Asia", *Journal of Contemporary Asia,* Vol. 9, No. 3, 1979, p. 274.
4. *Ibid.,* p. 279.
5. "Tourism and the Caribbean", *Science and Society,* Vol. XXXVII, Winter 1973-74, p. 475.
6. Turner, L. & Ash, J., *The Golden Hordes, op. cit.,* NY, 1976, p. 110.
7. Wood, *op. cit.,* p. 281.
8. *Op. cit.*
9. Pacific Islands Development Commission, *The Pacific Islands Tourism Conference,* 1973, p. 57.

Chapter 4
1. Francillon Gerhard, *Bali-Tourism, Culture, Environment*, Unesco, 1974.
2. Report in *Sunday Nation,* Singapore, 14 September 1975.
3. Report in *Straits Times,* Singapore, 28 October 1980.
4. *Pacific News Service,* 604 Mission Street, Room 1001, San Francisco, California, USA, monitors events relating to Hawaiian tourism.
5. Report in *Die Tageszeitung,* 16 June 1980.
6. International Workshop on Tourism, Report on Socio-cultural Effects.

Chapter 5
1. The best source of continuing information on the Japanese campaign against sexual tourism is *The Japan Christian Activity News,* published by the National Christian Council of Japan, Room 24, 2-3-18, Nishiwaseda, Shinjuku-ku, Tokyo 160, Japan, and *Asian Women's Liberation,* Asian Women's Association, c/- Ms Goto, 112 Sakuragaoka, Hodogaya-ku, Yokohama 240, Japan.
2. Moderator Ushiroku, *Kyodan Newsletter,* No. 158, 20 September 1981.
3. *Japan Christian Activity News,* No. 559, 21 March 1980.

Chapter 6
1. A summary of the current situation is contained in "Blue Sea, Golden Sand, Red Ink", *Far Eastern Economic Review,* 11 September 1981, p. 62.
2. *Travel Trade Gazette,* 9 February 1973.
3. Turner, L. & Ash, J., *The Golden Hordes, op. cit.,* p. 199-203.
4. *Third World Tourism,* Christian Conference of Asia, 1980, p. 35.

Chapter 7
1. Biddlecomb, Cynthia B., *Pacific Tourism,* PCC, Suva, Fiji, 1981, p. 51.
2. *Be My Guest,* Prentice-Hall, New York, 1957. "The inspiring saga of the man behind one of America's great success stories" (Sic).

Chapter 9
1. Saglio, C., "Tourism for Discovery: a Project in Lower Casamance, Senegal", *Tourism — Passport to Development,* Chapter 18, pp. 321-335.
2. *Ibid.,* p. 333.
3. *Tourism: the Asian Dilemma,* p. 47.

Appendices

APPENDIX 1
INTERNATIONAL WORKSHOP STATEMENT

The International Workshop on Tourism, sponsored by the Christian Conference of Asia, attended by 30 participants from 18 countries, was held in Manila, September 12-25, 1980.

The Workshop was convened primarily to assess and examine the phenomenon of international tourism particularly from a third world viewpoint.

The one most glaring thing that surfaced from the deliberations of the Workshop was that tourism wreaked more havoc than brought benefits to recipient third world countries.

From an historical perspective, third world countries have discovered time and time again how their economies, cultures and social structures have been disrupted by the long-term effects of tourism.

In its present format, linked as it is with transnational corporations, ruling elites and political hegemonies, and totally unmindful of the real spiritual, economic, political and socio-cultural needs of recipient countries, the Workshop seriously questioned whether tourism as it is could be salvaged.

Reports from delegates coming from different corners of the third world repeatedly exploded the myths of tourism being a foreign exchange earner, an employment booster, or an enhancer of cultural exchange between countries.

In the area of foreign exchange, what comes in as foreign exchange easily escapes via what is known as foreign exchange leakage. The real beneficiaries were not the poor recipient third world countries but the rich industrialized tourist-generating countries which control the entire industry — hotel cartels, airlines, tour operators and agencies.

The myth of tourism being an employment booster was shattered as investigations verified that, viewed against the total labour force of any given country, the jobs generated by tourism were minimal, seasonal and highly exploitative.

The World Bank and other financial institutions have a hand in including tourism in development programmes and giving it an unwarranted priority. Sharing culpability in the vicious cycle of loans and balance of payment crises are local elites, some of whom hold government posts, and thus facilitate such arrangements to their advantage.

As far as cultural exchange is concerned, this was also discovered to be largely a myth. Given the nature and short duration of a tourist's stay in a country, cultural exchange, if any, could only take place on a most superficial level. On the other hand, package tours from consumer-oriented countries tend to generate package culture, package sex, particularly those promoted by the Japanese and the presence of American bases.

If tourism is therefore to be salvaged, a thorough re-thinking and re-structuring of the whole industry is called for, taking as its basic premise, not profit-making and crass materialism, but the fundamental spiritual and human development of peoples everywhere.

Bearing this in mind, the Workshop explored the alternatives of people-oriented tourism, encounter-type travel and the non-exploitative kinds of tours where the local indigene, especially the workers, and the tourist alike would be the real beneficiaries.

Affirming its optimism in the ability of third world peoples to work out their own destinies and free themselves from unequal development programmes of which tourism is but one facet, the Workshop would like the World Tourism Organization and all people of good will to share in their search for a more humane international tourism.

APPENDIX 2
A BIBLICAL REFLECTION

Most of the events of the Bible took place within the thin corridor of land linking Europe, Asia, and Africa. It was the cross-roads of the ancient world. On the flat strip of land along the Palestine coast a natural land bridge gave access between Eurasia and Africa to a continual traffic of trade caravans, religious pilgrims, and foreign armies. The politics of the region were confused and at various periods were dominated by Egypt, Assyria, and Mesopotamia.

By the time of Christ, Imperial Rome had established sovereignty over Israel and developed an infrastructure of roads and ports, inns and trading centers as well as an efficient courier system for communications. The roads carried a heavy traffic especially at the time of the Jewish Passover when pilgrims descended on Jerusalem (Luke 2:41). Sometimes a census would add to the confusion (Luke 2:3–5).

Jerusalem and the main cities of Israel had the appearance of a modern tourist destination with a cosmopolitan atmosphere, many languages spoken, and a constant stream of people arriving and departing. The organization of such large numbers required a certain discipline, and this was provided by the laws of Moses, which gave clear rules about the reception of visitors, the conduct of travellers, and the obligations of the community.

The host

The Hebrews had been nomads and understood the special problems of travellers passing through an alien land, especially the cultural conflicts which emerge. In addition they had suffered a long period of captivity in Egypt and had experienced the indignity of oppression. The constant memory of slavery and liberation reinforced the enlightened code of laws which they developed. In this code the Hebrews attempted to provide a social structure which was non-aggressive and which sought the well-being of the stranger and sojourner as well as the Hebrew people. It was a brave experiment to establish a human community based on justice.

In relation to the stranger the basic rule was that he or she should not be molested but accepted as a member of the family with all the rights and privileges entailed. Visitors were to be fed, sheltered, and given provisions for their onward journey. The guest was inviolate.

> You must not oppress the stranger, you know how a stranger feels, for you lived as strangers in the land of Egypt [Exod. 23:9].

While it was the experience of oppression which gave the impetus for these humane laws, we must also recognize a strong element of self-interest in their implementation. In a volatile political situation each new generation had to grapple with the problem of national security. Showing compassion to the stranger now might ensure reciprocal treatment in the future. The hospitality of the Old Testament emerged as much from fear as from generosity.

To reinforce the importance of generosity to strangers the Hebrews developed the myth of the unknown stranger. This story is found in many other traditional societies. The Hebrew account begins with Abraham, who showed generous treatment to three strangers only to find, on their departure, that they were actually angels (Gen. 18:1-8). Two of the strangers then went to the home of Lot (himself a visitor in the region), and when local trouble-makers wanted to start a fight with the strangers, Lot intervened and made the remarkable offer of his own daughters for their pleasure rather than violate the strict rules governing his action as a host to guests. The angels rewarded Lot by rescuing him from the fiery end of Sodom (Gen. 19:1-6).

The warmth and extent of later Hebrew hospitality became legendary. The Queen of Sheba knew the reputation of Solomon (2 Chron. 9); David and Nehemiah were among those respected for their lavish hospitality (2 Sam. 9:7,8; Neh. 5:17f); the prostitute Rahab became a symbol of righteousness by caring for foreigners and refusing to surrender them to the military (Jos. 2:1-17); and the later prophets warned of the need to continue the practice:

Do not exploit the stranger [Jer. 22:3].
Do not rob the settler of his rights [Mal. 3:5].

Jesus inherited this tradition and was dependent on the hospitality of friends throughout his ministry. He developed the Old Testament idea by stating that to receive the stranger is to receive Christ himself. This strikingly germinal idea has been the motivation behind the actions of many of the saints of the church whose service to the people has derived from the recognition of Christ in the stranger. A constant theme in literature and poetry, it has become accepted in recent theology as the sign of Christ's presence among the poor and the marginalized strangers.

In the parable of the last judgment (Matt. 25:35), Jesus places hospitality in the center of the faith when he indicates that a part of God's judgment on us will be based on whether or not we open our doors to strangers.

The early church held to this same belief. Paul was insistent that "you should make hospitality your special care" (Rom. 12:13), and the writer to the Hebrews advised, "remember always to welcome strangers" (Heb. 13:2). When Paul listed the criteria for choosing the leaders of the early church, he included hospitality as one of the obligations (1 Tim. 3:2; Titus 1:8).

The Christian community became known for its generous treatment of visitors, and the Christians themselves became well-travelled as they spread their message from one country to another. But hospitality was not practiced for Christians alone, and any traveller was made welcome. A little-known incident illustrating the care of Christians for their community took place in Alexandria in 262 A.D. When plague struck the city, most of the inhabitants fled to safety, but the Christian community remained behind and opened their homes to the sick and the dying who were unable to leave. The church became known for its selfless service.

Throughout history a number of religious communities were established out of the need to provide hospitality to travellers and pilgrims and this obligation became fixed in the

Rule of St. Benedict. Most communities which have been centers for renewal owe their effectiveness to an open-door policy which has enabled fresh insights and challenges to come from the wisdom of visiting strangers.

The traveller

If the host had responsibilities before God, so too did the travellers, who were required to show sensitivity to the religious and social traditions of the host community. In Hebrew law the sojourner was obliged to respect both the religious rites (Lev. 20:2-5) and the laws governing the community (Lev. 18:26-28; 24:16). When Christ sent his disciples to the neighboring towns, he set down strict rules to govern their behavior (Mark 6:8-12; Matt. 10:9-14).

The traveller is always in a vulnerable position, unable to anticipate all the dangers of the journey whether they come from crime or lack of knowledge of the local customs. This vulnerability has an important side-effect since it creates a context in which conversion becomes possible. Human behavior is such that radical change is facilitated by being exposed to an uncertain or hostile environment. Maximized uncertainty becomes the prelude to conversion. This is exemplified by the number of profound religious revelations which have come to people as they journeyed in unfamiliar surroundings.

The Bible is replete with examples of this phenomenon. Abraham encountered God's providence and promise in his journeys (Gen. 15); Jacob discovered God's presence while journeying to Haran (Gen. 28:1-22); on the seven-mile journey from Jerusalem to Emmaus two men encountered the risen Christ (Luke 24:13-35); and Paul was converted by a blinding light on the Damascus Road (Acts 9:1-9).

The road is the symbol of religious discovery. Leaders of faith from Buddha to Mohammed and from St. Francis of Assisi to Mahatma Gandhi experienced the holy while journeying from one point to another.

In our own life many of us have known similar, but less

dramatic experiences. To travel a new road is always to expose one's own life to the unexpected and the holy. We confront a series of new social and cultural forces which make us question some long-held but seldom-examined assumptions about life. On the road we discover the human face of the stranger and meet our own stranger within.

Once we drop our cultural arrogance and enter into dialogue with people of another culture in a spirit of humility, unexpected things will occur. Our racial blindness can be challenged by meeting persons of another race, and our religious imperialism is threatened when we meet holiness in a person of another faith.

Such encounters are not all positive and sometimes prejudice is reinforced. Travel always has risk and danger. The man who journeyed alone from Jerusalem to Jericho was mugged by robbers, lost all his luggage, and was badly beaten up (Luke 10:29f). Yet even this unpleasant experience exposed him not only to human cruelty but also to human kindness. He learned a new respect for the despised Samaritan, who was the only one to come to his rescue. Possibly he also found some new insights into his own prejudice and behavior.

To travel with an open spirit is to expose oneself to the chance of growth, the danger of loss, and the possibility of conversion.

The contradiction

The modern world has seen the growth of widespread travel by relatively rich people to the land of predominantly poor people, with the sole motivation of pleasure on the part of the rich. The size of this movement has no historical precedent, and it has no possible justification in either biblical or theological terms. The inherent hedonism of such travel in countries where poverty is rampant makes a mockery of the poor and cannot be part of a Christian lifestyle.

A parable of Jesus speaks to this situation. In the story there is a wealthy man named Lazarus, and each day he passes a poor beggar sitting at his front gate. The poor man, covered with sores, is simply an object. He occasions neither the compassion of Lazarus nor does he constitute a challenge to the rich man's lifestyle. He is a non-person. In the reversal at the conclusion of the story, both men die and Lazarus learns what it means to be poor, miserable, and oppressed and the poor man is rewarded.

In their travel to poor nations, tourists literally act out this same parable every day. As they leave their comfortable, air-conditioned hotels to go to the tour bus, they step over the same poor man, still covered with sores and still sitting at the entrance waiting for compassion. After a few days, the tourist becomes like Lazarus and looks through the poor man. He is simply a part of the background, possibly even the subject for a photograph, and the conscience of the tourist will be appeased by the scattering of a few coins. The tourist who can live in such a compromising situation where the cost of one night's accommodation in a hotel exceeds the monthly salary of the average citizen of the host country has dulled his or her sensitivity to the suffering of the people.

Relationship

At the heart of the gospel is the imperative to establish right human relationships, summarized by the full meaning of the word "love." Christians are called to love their neighbor as themselves, to cultivate the habit of love and to act toward all people, even their enemies, in a spirit of love. Love is not an ethereal emotion but a relationship based on justice. Christians work for a society where there is justice in the relationships between persons of every race, creed, language, culture, social class, age, and between male and female.

When tourism is examined in the light of this understanding of the gospel it shows an ambivalent face. Travel has provided the context in which many people have discovered a whole new world of love and justice and have come to a new and profoundly rich understanding of the *oikoumene* (the whole inhabited earth). Human relationships built up in this way have been among the strongest influences on our life. We would covet this experience for others. However, the gain in human relations must not be at the expense of creating or perpetuating structures of injustice.

Again we have to distinguish between tourism where both host and guest have an approximately equivalent level of wealth and that situation in which the tourist's wealth far exceeds that of the local people. In the former situation, tourism certainly has the potential to improve human relations through international understanding in a way which does not have too many negative effects on the structure of society.

It is a different situation when the rich tourists visit the poor nations. The relationship between host and guest becomes entirely commercial. It can never become the meeting of equals since one partner holds the dominant power which comes from the possession of money.

In the account of the early Church, a rich man approached Peter the apostle and offered to buy from him the gift of healing. Peter's angry reply was, "May your silver be lost forever, and you with it, for thinking that money could buy what God has given for nothing!" (Acts 8:20). There is a parallel between this incident and the tourist who attempts to purchase a relationship with money. A relationship dependent solely or even primarily on the financial superiority of one person can never become a just relationship.

Christians in both host nations and tourist-sending countries can help to create an environment in which tourism will be redeemed and will create social relationships of love and justice where people can meet as equals and develop their full human potential.

These are big words and large ideals. Behind them lies the very simple encounter of two people across the boundaries which divide their different worlds, a meeting in which a new relationship of trust and love can be established. This is the promise of tourism and this is the ideal which the Indian poet Rabindranath Tagore has described so well:

Thou hast made me known to friends whom I knew not,
given me seats in homes not my own.
Thou hast brought the distant near
and made me a brother of the stranger.

APPENDIX 3
RESOURCES

The Ecumenical Coalition on Third World Tourism
c/o Office for Human Development
Dona Matilde Building 301
876 G. Apacible Ermita, Manila
Philippines

Founded in 1981 as a result of the International Workshop on Tourism, the Coalition now has official support from the Federation of Asian Bishops Conference (FABC), the Christian Conference of Asia (CCA), the Pacific Conference of Churches (PCC) and the Caribbean Conference of Churches (CCC). It undertakes to monitor tourism effects from a third world Christian perspective.

Publications:
Third World Tourism, Report on the International Workshop, ed. Ron O'Grady, CCA, 1980.
Parker Rossman, "Tourism: an Issue for the Churches", *Christian Century*, 21 January 1981, p. 54.

World Council of Churches
150 route de Ferney
1211 Geneva 20
Switzerland

Has no specific department dealing with tourism, but enquiries can go to the Laity Department.

Publications:
Leisure-Tourism: Threat and Promise, ed. Ian M. Fraser, 1970.
"Participation in Change — Tourism the Two-edged Sword", *Study Encounter*, Vol. VIII, No. 2, 1972.

The Pontifical Pastoral Commission for Migration and Tourism
Palazzo San Calisto
Rome
Italy

The task of the Commission is primarily Pastoral and educational although it has recently begun to show concern for wider issues. In

May 1978 the Commission held a pastoral conference on tourism.

Publication:
The Church and Mankind on the Move, 1978.

Christian Conference of Asia
480 Lorong 2
Toa Payoh,
Singapore 1231

The CCA conducted a research programme on Asian tourism in 1975. It followed this with some local activities, and in 1980 sponsored the International Workshop on Tourism held in Manila, Philippines.

Publication:
Tourism: the Asian Dilemma, Ed. Ron O'Grady, 1975.

The Pacific Conference of Churches
P.O. Box 208
Suva
Fiji

Through its commission on Church and Society it has produced several documents and held seminars on Pacific tourism.

Publication:
Cynthia Z. Biddlecomb, *Pacific Tourism: Contrasts in Values and Expectations,* 1981.

Caribbean Conference of Churches
154 Charlotte Street
Port of Spain
P.O. Box 176
Trinidad

The Development Commission of the CCC has run seminars and supported several programmes to work with Caribbean tourism.

Publication:
The Role of Tourism in Caribbean Development, report of an ecumenical consultation, CADEC, Barbados, 1972.

Government agency
World Tourism Organization
Capitan Haya, 42
Madrid 20
Spain

The WTO is an organization of 107 governments plus 140 affiliate member organizations. Its aim is to "promote and develop tourism with a view to contributing to economic development, to international understanding, to peace, prosperity and universal respect for, and observance of, human rights and fundamental freedoms for all without distinction as to race, sex, language or religion." In October 1980 the world tourism conference of WTO adopted 'The Manila Declaration' which has a strong emphasis on the development of social, cultural and spiritual benefits from tourism.

Other resources
Among the books which give some useful background are the following:

de Kadt, Emanuel, *Tourism - Passport to Development?*, Report of a joint UNESCO-World Bank Seminar, OUP, New York, 1979.

Haden-Guest, Anthony, *Down the Programmed Rabbit-hole*, Granada, London, 1972.

Mendis, E.D.L, *The Economic, Social and Cultural Impact of Tourism in Sri Lanka*, CWF, Colombo, 1981.

Rivers, Patrick, *The Restless Generation*, Davis Poynter, London, 1972.

Smith, Valene E. ed., *Hosts and Guests*: the Anthropology of Tourism, University of Pennsylvania, 1977.

Turner, Louis and Ash, John, *The Golden Hordes: International Tourism and the Pleasure Periphery*; St Martins, NY, 1976.

Young, George, *Tourism: Blessing or Blight?*, Penguin, UK, 1973.